Lorna's beautifully written words convey a kind, merciful, and loving God. Daily taking time to mediate on our Creator strengthens our inner being and increases hope.

—Cecilia Quist, Mental Health Therapist
Lac La Biche, Alberta

Lorna's devotional is a collection of scripture verses and teachings straight from the heart of God to you. Lorna's prophetic insights have helped and encouraged everyone who knows her, so I know each page in this book will delight and strengthen you in the same way. Jeremiah 15:16 (AMP) says, *"Your words were found and I ate them, and Your words became a joy to me and the delight of my heart…"*

—Debbie Lee, Teacher
Lifeway Christian Academy, Saskatoon, Saskatchewan

My family has had a close relationship with the Hanishewski family for many years, and Lorna has always been a pillar of strength, in the midst of hard times as well as good times. She has faced some difficult challenges in life, and her response has always been to turn to God. It has been a blessing to see the stability, joy, care and compassion that Lorna displays in her life, her family and her ministry.

These *Devotions of the Heart* are born out of a life lived in dependency on our Saviour who we can always look to no matter what the need. As you read, you will have the opportunity to take in what God has shown her and the lessons she has learned in both the valleys and on the mountaintops!

—Brad Mayer
Evangelist, Canadian Fire Missions

BOOK 2

Devotions
of the ♥

Lorna Hanishewski

DEVOTIONS OF THE HEART, VOLUME TWO
Copyright © 2019 by Lorna Hanishewski

All rights reserved. Neither this publication nor any part of this publication may be reproduced or transmitted in any form or by any means, electronic or mechanical, including photocopying, recording or any information storage and retrieval system, without permission in writing from the author.

Scripture marked AMP taken from the Amplified® Bible, Copyright © 2015 by The Lockman Foundation, La Habra, CA 90631. All rights reserved. • Scripture marked AMPC taken from the Amplified® Bible, Classic Edition, Copyright © 1954, 1958, 1962, 1964, 1965, 1987 by The Lockman Foundation. Used by permission. • Scripture marked CEB taken from the Common English Bible, Copyright © 2011 by Common English Bible. • Scripture marked CEV taken from the Contemporary English Version, Copyright © 1991, 1992, 1995 by American Bible Society, Used by Permission. • Scripture marked DARBY taken from the Darby translation, which is in the public domain. • Scripture marked ESV taken from The Holy Bible, English Standard Version® (ESV®), Copyright © 2001 by Crossway, a publishing ministry of Good News Publishers. Used by permission. All rights reserved. • Scripture marked GNT taken from the Good News Translation, Copyright © 1992 by American Bible Society. • Scripture marked GW taken from the GOD's WORD Translation, Copyright © 1995 by God's Word to the Nations. Used by permission of Baker Publishing Group. • Scripture marked HCSB taken from the Holman Christian Standard Bible, Copyright © 1999, 2000, 2002, 2003, 2009 by Holman Bible Publishers, Nashville Tennessee. All rights reserved. • Scripture marked ICB taken from The Holy Bible, International Children's Bible® Copyright© 1986, 1988, 1999, 2015 by Tommy Nelson™, a division of Thomas Nelson. Used by permission. • Scripture marked JUB taken from the Jubilee Bible 2000, Copyright © 2000, 2001, 2010 by Life Sentence Publishing, Inc. • Scripture marked KJV taken from the King James version, which is in the public domain. • Scripture marked MEV taken from The Holy Bible, Modern English Version. Copyright © 2014 by Military Bible Association. Published and distributed by Charisma House. • Scripture marked MSG taken from The Message, Copyright © 1993, 1994, 1995, 1996, 2000, 2001, 2002 by Eugene H. Peterson. • Scripture marked NABRE taken from the New American Bible, revised edition © 2010, 1991, 1986, 1970 Confraternity of Christian Doctrine, Inc., Washington, DC All Rights Reserved. • Scripture marked NASB taken from the New American Standard Bible, Copyright © 1960, 1962, 1963, 1968, 1971, 1972, 1973, 1975, 1977, 1995 by The Lockman Foundation. • Scripture marked NCV taken from The Holy Bible, New Century Version®, Copyright © 2005 by Thomas Nelson, Inc. • Scripture marked NET taken from the New English Translation, NET Bible®, Copyright ©1996-2006 by Biblical Studies Press, L.L.C. http://netbible.com All rights reserved. • Scripture marked NIRV taken from The Holy Bible, New International Reader's Version, Copyright © 1995, 1996, 1998, 2014 by Biblica, Inc.®. Used by permission. All rights reserved worldwide. • Scripture marked NIV taken from The Holy Bible, New International Version®, NIV® Copyright ©1973, 1978, 1984, 2011 by Biblica, Inc.® Used by permission. All rights reserved worldwide. • Scripture marked NKJV taken from the New King James Version®, Copyright © 1982 by Thomas Nelson, Inc. Used by permission. All rights reserved. • Scripture marked NLT taken from the Holy Bible, New Living Translation, Copyright ©1996, 2004, 2007 by Tyndale House Foundation. Used by permission of Tyndale House Publishers, Inc., Carol Stream, Illinois 60188. All rights reserved. • Scripture marked TPT taken from The Passion Translation®, Copyright © 2017 by BroadStreet Publishing® Group, LLC. Used by permission. All rights reserved. thePassionTranslation.com

Printed in Canada

Print ISBN: 978-1-4866-1783-8
eBook ISBN: 978-1-4866-1784-5

Word Alive Press
119 De Baets Street Winnipeg, MB R2J 3R9
www.wordalivepress.ca

MIX
Paper from responsible sources
FSC® C103567

WORD ALIVE
—P R E S S—

Cataloguing in Publication information can be obtained from Library and Archives Canada.

I would like to dedicate this book to my children, their spouses, and my grandchildren. I love you all!

Children are God's love-gift; they are heaven's generous reward. (Psalm 127:3, TPT)

I would also like to dedicate it in loving memory of my mom, Erma Ileen Gardner, September 7, 1935–October 3, 2018, who is now enjoying her heavenly reward.

ACKNOWLEDGEMENTS

With a grateful heart, I would like to thank and acknowledge Pastor Catherine Randall for her continual encouragement in my writing of this book. Catherine, thank you for collecting together reflections and devotions that I had previously written and exhorting me to rewrite them into a book. I'm also grateful for the many, many hours you spent assisting me in checking the accuracy of scripture and readability of the manuscript. You have gone above and beyond with your help and encouragement. I thank God for you. You are a dear and precious friend. May many blessings abound to your account.

FOREWORD

I've known Lorna for over thirty years and I have to say that she is one of the most positive, joy-filled people I know! She has faced difficult moments with remarkable grace and peace, and Lorna's ability to hear God's voice in the everyday moments of life has been a blessing to me on so many occasions. Many years ago as I taught on prayer in a children's class, I asked the kids what they wanted to agree on in prayer. The answer was unanimous—they wanted a party, so we prayed together for just that. The very same day Lorna told me that the thought had come to her to have a party in class. I realized that at the time we'd agreed in prayer in the morning service, Lorna had heard God's encouragement to give the children a party in class. I can't tell you how often such moments have happened throughout the years of our friendship.

In recent years, Lorna began posting daily on Facebook and many friends liked or commented on what she had written. It became obvious that her posts were engaging people in a deep way. Her unshakeable trust in God's goodness and her ability to hear Him in the most difficult time of her life blessed and encouraged so many people. Over time, many responded by saying "Lorna, you should write a devotional book," and the idea was born. We realized that she had already written her devotional on Facebook, and we just needed to put it into book format. We've spent much time together getting it ready, and it's been a fun, inspiring, and exciting process to finally see it go to print!

I pray that many are blessed and encouraged and gain a desire to grow closer to God through reading your devotions, Lorna! Well done! You're an inspiration to us all!

(P.S. Lorna, did you notice all the exclamation marks?)

—Pastor Catherine Randall
City Centre Church, Saskatoon, Saskatchewan

AUTHOR'S NOTE

Dear Readers,
I pray these devotions will encourage and bless you, inspiring you to grow in your relationship with God. They have arisen out of my own personal times with the Lord, and they draw on what He has revealed and taught me over the past several years—a time in which He has brought me joyfully through a very difficult and challenging season of my life.

This volume represents the second half of a year's worth of devotions, and is meant to be read in conjunction with Volume One.

Your sister in Christ,
Lorna

Devotional

DAY 182

Renew Your Mind

I like the Psalms because they teach us how to encourage ourselves in the Lord. The Word of God illuminates, bringing us revelation and understanding as we choose to renew our minds each day.

Your word is a lamp to my feet and a light to my path. (Psalm 119:105, NKJV)

Paul talks about putting on the armour of God so we can fight against the strategies of the enemy; he tells us to take up the sword of the Spirit, which is the Word of God. When we renew our mind, it helps us to think right. Wrong thinking produces wrong actions, but right thinking produces right actions.

They are double-minded, unstable in all their ways. (James 1:8, CEB)

We cannot be full of joy and despair, or peace and fear, at the same. We must use the sword of the Spirit to stand against the attacks of the enemy. The devil is not a roaring lion, but a fake who pretends so he can seek and devour. The enemy cannot devour those who are strong in the Lord and the power of His might. The Word of God will always bring hope!

Why, my soul, are you downcast? Why so disturbed within me? Put your hope in God, for I will yet praise him, my Savior and my God. (Psalm 42:11, NIV)

…but I have put my hope in your word. (Psalm 119:81b, NLT)

The Word of God will always prove true; it will stand forever—it does not change. We must choose to allow the Word to change our minds and renew our thinking.

DAY 183

Irresistible

I had a desire while praying one evening: that the Church would become irresistible to the unsaved. I looked up the word "irresistible" in the Oxford Dictionary, and it gave the perfect description: "Too attractive and tempting to be resisted."[1] How do we become irresistible to the world? I believe through the overflow of God's glory and presence in our lives. The world will say, "What is it about you? I want what you have."

As I continued to pray, I saw a painter prepared with a roller and dazzling white paint in front of an unpainted wall. I realized that the wall represents the Church, and its painter is the Lord. He will regenerate, rejuvenate, remodel, and refresh us with His glory, causing us to become a repentant people; pure, holy, without spot or blemish, ready for the coming of the Lord, and irresistible to the world.

> *Repent therefore and be converted, that your sins may be blotted out, so that times of refreshing may come from the presence of the Lord, and that He may send Jesus Christ, who was preached to you before, whom heaven must receive until the times of restoration of all things, which God has spoken by the mouth of all His holy prophets since the world began.* (Acts 3:19–21, NKJV)

DAY 184

Praise Brings Victory

Praise has helped me get through many storms in life. I have learned that praise silences the enemy and brings victory. The one voice that will always be heard above the storm is the voice of praise.

> *But at midnight Paul and Silas were praying and singing hymns to God, and the prisoners were listening to them. Suddenly there was a great earthquake, so that the foundations of the prison were shaken; and immediately all the doors were opened and everyone's chains were loosed. And the keeper of the prison, awaking from sleep and seeing the prison doors open, supposing the prisoners had fled, drew his sword and was about to kill himself. But Paul called with a loud voice, saying, "Do yourself no harm, for we are all here."*
>
> *Then he called for a light, ran in, and fell down trembling before Paul and Silas. And he brought them out and said "Sirs, what must I do to be saved?"* (Acts 16:25–30, NKJV)

The story of Paul and Silas is a great example of how praise brings victory. They were in a horrible situation: beaten, put in stocks, and left in the dungeon, all because they had set a girl free of a demonic spirit. Instead of feeling sorry for themselves or having a wrong attitude, they began to sing and praise their God. God sent an earthquake and set Paul and Silas and all the other prisoners free!

Praise brings freedom from bondage—not only to the ones praising, but to those caught up in the same atmosphere. The prisoners, as well as the jailer and his household, reaped the benefit of Paul and Silas's praise. Praise is a powerful force!

DAY 185

Anointed

God has given us His Spirit so we can help others. We are clothed in His righteousness, and therefore anointed and able to preach the Word to others, to bring them to a saving knowledge of Jesus Christ that He may be glorified.

> *The Sovereign Lord has filled me with his Spirit. He has chosen me and sent me to bring good news to the poor, To heal the brokenhearted, To announce release to captives and freedom to those in prison. He has sent me to proclaim that the time has come when the Lord will save his people and defeat their enemies. He has sent me to comfort all who mourn, To give to those who mourn in Zion joy and gladness instead of grief, A song of praise instead of sorrow. They will be like trees that the Lord himself has planted. They will all do what is right, And God will be praised for what he has done. They will rebuild cities that have long been in ruins.*
>
> *My people, foreigners will serve you. They will take care of your flocks and farm your land and tend your vineyards. And you will be known as the priests of the Lord, The servants of our God. You will enjoy the wealth of the nations and be proud that it is yours. Your shame and disgrace are ended. You will live in your own land, And your wealth will be doubled; Your joy will last forever.*
>
> *The Lord says, "I love justice and I hate oppression and crime. I will faithfully reward my people and make an eternal covenant with them."* (Isaiah 61:1–8, GNT)

God is speaking to Israel, but this message is just as much for us today who have been grafted in.

Jerusalem rejoices because of what the Lord has done. She is like a bride dressed for her wedding. God has clothed her with salvation and victory. (Isaiah 61:10, GNT)

We are so blessed to be called children of God, and to be anointed to share the Good News!

DAY 186

A Song of Praise

The Holy Spirit is a singing Spirit, and He puts a song in our hearts. If we allow Him to rise up in us, we will always have a song of praise on our lips. It may be a song that someone else has written or it may come out of our own spirits, but when we begin to sing, the atmosphere changes outside and inside. It will take us higher and deeper in Him.

> *O Lord, I will always sing of your constant love; I will proclaim your faithfulness forever. I know that your love will last for all time, that your faithfulness is as permanent as the sky....*
>
> *The heavens sing of the wonderful things you do; the holy ones sing of your faithfulness, Lord. No one in heaven is like you, Lord; none of the heavenly beings is your equal. You are feared in the council of the holy ones; they all stand in awe of you.*
>
> *Lord God Almighty, none is as mighty as you; in all things you are faithful, O Lord....*
>
> *How powerful you are! How great is your strength! Your kingdom is founded on righteousness and justice; love and faithfulness are shown in all you do.*
>
> *How happy are the people who worship you with songs, who live in the light of your kindness! Because of you they rejoice all day long, and they praise you for your goodness. You give us great victories; in your love you make us triumphant.* (Psalm 89:1–2, 5–8, 13–17, GNT)

DAY 187

Choose to Praise

I enjoy being at home, even though it can be lonely at times. One day I was alone and I began praising God. In times like that, it seems we are more open to hearing God speak. As I was praising God, this thought came to me: "Being a singer doesn't make you a praiser!" A singer can sing without praising, but a praiser cannot praise without singing. Making a joyful noise unto the Lord may not sound good to man, but it always sounds good to God, and it's a powerful weapon that sends the enemy fleeing.

> *Always be joyful. Never stop praying. Whatever happens, give thanks, because it is God's will in Christ Jesus that you do this.* (1 Thessalonians 5:16–17, GW)

This is a very special verse that God emphasized to me before I went on my missions trip to Kenya. I thought it was something He wanted me to share with the people there, but it became apparent that I needed the comfort, strength, and direction it provided when suddenly faced with the tragic death of my husband. Always be joyful, pray, and give thanks—no matter what happens. We must put on the garment of praise, and choose each day to be more than just a singer—be a praiser instead!

DAY 188

Entirely Faithful

O Lord God of Heaven's Armies! Where is there anyone as mighty as you, O Lord? You are entirely faithful. (Psalm 89:8, NLT)

No one is entirely faithful except for God, but we can learn to be faithful in many things. We may try our best, but we will never be completely faithful because we have not been perfected. However, God is completely perfect and entirely reliable. Wordreference.com defines "entirely" as "wholly or fully; completely or unreservedly; solely or exclusively."[2] Our God is entirely, exclusively, completely—in other words, without question—totally faithful to His Word. We can totally depend on God to do what He says. Even if something doesn't work out the way we think it should, the problem is usually ours, not God's. I love the words in the song "The Steadfast Love of the Lord" by Edith McNeill. The Bible refers to this as well in the book of Lamentations:

Through the Lord's mercies we are not consumed, Because His compassions fail not. They are new every morning; Great is Your faithfulness. (Lamentations 3:22–23, NKJV)

DAY 189

All Is Well with My Soul

There is nothing more wonderful than to know and understand deeply that all is well with your soul!

Consider it pure joy, my brothers and sisters, whenever you face trials of many kinds… (James 1:2, NIV)

I was in Kenya on my birthday, and had finished an amazing day of ministry with two hundred children. I had just gone to bed when I overheard Pastor Edith say in another room, "Okay, I will give the phone to her," and then she passed it to my friend Pat. After Pat spoke, she said it was for me. It was my pastor's wife with the news of my husband's death.

My first reaction to the news was total shock, and I remember experiencing many different emotions—everything from fear to anger and to sadness. As I sat in a fog of emotion, I clearly heard God speak to me and say, "Just praise Me." Then I made a choice to rejoice and say, "All is well." I could have stayed angry and full of fear, thinking "Why did this terrible thing happen?" But I realized instantly that this had nothing to do with God. No matter what had happened or happens in the future, God is good!

I made a choice to rejoice and not to allow the devil to win, because Jesus came to give abundant life. We need to always be thankful, knowing that those who die in Christ, no matter the circumstances, are in the presence of the Lord. So rejoice, for all is well!

Rejoice always, pray continually, give thanks in all circumstances; for this is God's will for you in Christ Jesus. (1 Thessalonians 5:16–18, NIV)

The strength we find to endure and carry on during such times only comes from the Maker of heaven and earth. He carried our pain, sorrow, and grief so we don't have to. There is nothing we can't get through if we remember who is with us. I can say "All is well with my soul" because of my Saviour Jesus.

DAY 190

Pursue Me

Several months ago, the Lord was speaking to me about my pursuit of Him. I was recently reminded of it again because of a guest speaker talking about our desire for God. When the Lord first talked to me about this, He used the example of a hound dog: it pursues through the rain, heat, hills, rivers, and forests until it catches its prey. If we truly desire God, we will pursue Him like a hound dog goes after its prey.

We need to be in relentless pursuit of the Lord—in other words, consistent and intense, continual and ongoing. Do you want to overcome in life? If so, let your desire for God cause you to pursue Him relentlessly.

> *Then He said to them all, "If anyone desires to come after Me, let him deny himself, and take up his cross daily, and follow Me."* (Luke 9:23, NKJV)

DAY 191

God's Filling Station

God's presence is just like a gas station that is open twenty-four hours a day, seven days a week—only better! God's filling station never shuts down for any reason, and the gas is always free. You can fill up anytime you want, because through God's presence you have a direct line to heaven. You will receive power and strength to endure and to overcome. You will be filled to overflowing with love, joy, peace and boldness in the Holy Ghost.

> *Listen! Whoever is thirsty, come to the water! Whoever has no money can come, buy, and eat! Come, buy wine and milk. You don't have to pay; it's free!* (Isaiah 55:1, GW)

DAY 192

Don't Lose Your Song

As I was driving home, I was overwhelmed thinking about the goodness of God. I am so thankful He has put a song in my heart to sing when I need it most. There isn't a trial we can't overcome if we don't lose our song.

A guest speaker at my church spoke of our need to have a song in our hearts, and I began crying—not out of sadness, but because it touched my heart deeply. I had personally experienced the benefit of having a song in my heart. Praising God helps us through difficulties and moves us forward in life. It may seem opposite to what seems natural, but our first response to any difficult situation should be to praise God. I began to sing loudly:

> *Oh, give thanks to the Lord, for He is good! For His mercy endures forever. Let the redeemed of the Lord say so, Whom He has redeemed from the hand of the enemy.* (Psalm 107:1–2, NKJV)

DAY 193

Is it Well with You?

I can't stop singing the old hymn written by Horatio Spafford, "It Is Well with My Soul."

When peace like a river attendeth my way,
When sorrows like sea billows roll,
Whatever my lot, Thou hast taught me to say,
"It is well, it is well with my soul."
But Lord, 'tis for Thee, for Thy coming we wait,
The sky, not the grave is our goal;
Oh trump of the angel! Oh voice of the Lord!
Blessed hope, blessed rest of my soul!
And Lord haste the day when the faith shall be sight,
The clouds be rolled back as a scroll;
The trump shall resound, and the Lord shall descend,
Even so, it is well with my soul.

The song reminds me of the story about the Shunammite woman. Her son died, so she went to find Elisha. When Elisha saw her coming, he told his servant to go and ask her if all was well. Her first response, even though her son had died, was to say, "It is well!" That's the same response we need to have, because no matter the situation, we have the victory—even over death.

> *So it was, when the man of God saw her afar off, that he said to his servant Gehazi, "Look, the Shunammite woman! Please run now to meet her, and say to her, 'Is it well with you? Is it well with your husband? Is it well with your child?'"*
> *And she answered, "It is well."* (2 Kings 4:25b–26, NKJV)

DAY 194

Plugged In

Oh, the joy of God's presence! There is no power outage or shortage with God—we can plug into His power source anytime. When I lived on an acreage, the power would go off quite often. Even if I hadn't been home, I would know it had been off because all the clocks would be flashing. I was told that the brownouts were because of the increase of power usage due to population growth.

Not so with the Lord! The more of us that gather together, the stronger and more powerful our connection to God becomes. How do we plug in to God's power? We enter with thanksgiving and praise continually.

> *I will bless the Lord at all times; His praise shall continually be in my mouth.* (Psalm 34:1, NKJV)

If the Bible tells us to rejoice always, pray continually, and give thanks in everything, then we can learn to do it as a lifestyle. This should be our goal. It will keep us plugged into God, and everything else we do will flow out of His presence.

DAY 195

Mountains Will Melt

A thought came to me from the Bible: "Mountains and hills will melt in the presence of the Lord." We need to think about what the mountains are in our lives, and allow them to be removed when we are in His presence. No matter how big the issues are, they will melt away in God's presence—problems like addictions, fear, anxiety, anger, bitterness, unforgiveness, oppression, and depression. Thank God for the victory we have in Him!

> *The Lord rules as king. Let the earth rejoice. Let all the islands be joyful. Clouds and darkness surround him. Righteousness and justice are the foundations of his throne. Fire spreads ahead of him. It burns his enemies who surround him. His flashes of lightning light up the world. The earth sees them and trembles. The mountains melt like wax in the presence of the Lord, in the presence of the Lord of the whole earth. The heavens tell about his righteousness, and all the people of the world see his glory.* (Psalm 97:1–6, GW)

DAY 196

Rev Up Your Engine

Before I was a Christian, I used to go to drink at the bar, where it was common for people to have shots of straight alcohol. As Christians, we need a shot of the Holy Ghost! Just as most drinking isn't done alone, we need to drink of the Spirit as we gather on Sunday mornings, or for prayer, teaching, Bible study, or praise and worship services. We all need a boost, and like a car, it can't be done alone. More than one car is required.

Make sure your life is getting an energy boost from the Spirit of God, and drink of the Spirit. We will find our life charged and revved up to overcome! Praise God!

Don't destroy yourself by getting drunk, but let the Spirit fill your life. When you meet together, sing psalms, hymns, and spiritual songs, as you praise the Lord with all your heart. Always use the name of our Lord Jesus Christ to thank God the Father for everything. (Ephesians 5:18–19, CEV)

Let the teaching of Christ live in you richly. Use all wisdom to teach and instruct each other by singing psalms, hymns, and spiritual songs with thankfulness in your hearts to God. (Colossians 3:16, NCV)

DAY 197

Light Disperses Darkness

The deeper the darkness is in a person's life, the brighter the light will shine upon their deliverance.

The people who walked in darkness have seen a great light… (Isaiah 9:2a, NKJV)

The people who sat in darkness have seen a great light… (Matthew 4:16a, NKJV)

The story of Saul on the road to Damascus is a good example of this. He thought he was doing right, but in reality, he was in a great darkness—he was blind spiritually. When we allow the Lord entrance into our lives, His light will disperse the darkness: deception, fear, anxiety, worry, depression, anger, offence, bitterness, hate, prejudice, rejection, addictions, sickness, loneliness, grief, and sorrow. The glory of God's presence in our lives outshines any darkness and replaces it with peace, joy and love.

Arise, shine; For your light has come! And the glory of the Lord is risen upon you. For behold, the darkness shall cover the earth, And deep darkness the people; But the Lord will arise over you, And His glory will be seen upon you. (Isaiah 60:1–2, NKJV)

DAY 198

The Condition of Our Heart

Our world is coloured by the condition of our heart. It's like seeing through colour-tinted glasses. We need healing, because past hurts alter the way we see—and Jesus is the only one who can heal a wounded soul.

The Word tells us that Jesus heals broken hearts and binds up our wounds. The story of the Good Samaritan is a great example, because he pours oil and wine on the wounds of the injured man. Oil and wine are representative of the Holy Spirit, who will heal the broken-hearted. When we reach out with compassion like the Samaritan did, the love of God in us will be poured out on the hurting. The Good Samaritan brought the injured man to an inn to be cared for. When we, as believers, act in love towards others, it will encourage them to come to the house of God, where they can encounter His presence and be healed and cared for.

> *…God's love has been poured out in our hearts through the Holy Spirit who has been given to us.* (Romans 5:5b, AMPC)

As Christians, with the help of the Holy Spirit the Lord wants us to minister healing to those who are wounded and broken-hearted. These are not only unbelievers—there are many in the body of Christ who are wounded and in need of healing. We need to press into God's presence and let Him pour His healing oil and wine into our lives—then we will be able to reach out to a hurting world.

DAY 199

Times and Seasons Change

Times and seasons change throughout life, so we often find ourselves entering or leaving a season, whether a spiritual or natural one. New seasons are always busy and challenging, but when you are faced with an abrupt change the challenge is heightened and intensified dramatically. The unknown can cause fear, but we need to do as God told Joshua:

> *Have I not commanded you? Be strong and of good courage; do not be afraid, nor be dismayed, for the Lord your God is with you wherever you go.* (Joshua 1:9, NKJV)

We need to learn to move into new seasons with confidence, knowing that God is with us. Be courageous as you step into new places spiritually and move out into uncharted waters. Let go of all doubt and fear as His grace and mercy surround you. His love and joy will abound in your heart, and His peace will fill your soul. All is well!

DAY 200

Embrace the New and Let Go of the Old

We don't have to fear, because the Lord is always near. Just let the Lord take your hand as you step out of the boat onto the water. You won't sink—you'll float on the waves of the Holy Ghost. Our responsibility is to take God at His word, so remember that wherever we go, He has promised to be there. Embracing the new is very necessary because faith is progressive, just as walking or running are forward motions. Even though our faith will be challenged, we need to embrace the new and let go of the old.

> *I admit that I haven't yet acquired the absolute fullness that I'm pursuing, but I run with passion into his abundance so that I may reach the purpose that Jesus Christ has called me to fulfill and wants me to discover. I don't depend on my own strength to accomplish this; however I do have one compelling focus: I forget all of the past as I fasten my heart to the future instead. I run straight for the divine invitation of reaching the heavenly goal and gaining the victory-prize through the anointing of Jesus.* (Philippians 3:13–14, TPT)

As we progress through every season, the future is bright—because it's filled with His ever-constant presence!

DAY 201

Faith Has a Sound

Recently at a praise night at my church, something really made a big impact on me. Sometimes we hear something but we haven't truly processed it, and that's what happened to me. The statement "Faith has a sound" suddenly became very real to me. I have heard and sung that line many times, but this time I understood that faith has a sound!

Faith cannot keep silent: it praises, shouts, dances, and declares! I thought of biblical characters who displayed this truth. David always had a song in his heart; Miriam sang and danced with the tambourine; blind Bartimaeus loudly cried out; the woman with the issue of blood kept speaking out loud to herself; and Paul and Silas sang in prison: all because faith has a sound. Is the sound you are making one of faith or is it filled with doubt? Make sure you're making a sound that can't be ignored. Don't let the enemy steal your faith!

Joyfully sing to the Lord, you righteous people. Praising the Lord is proper for decent people. Give thanks with a lyre to the Lord. Make music for him on a ten-stringed harp. Sing a new song to him. Play beautifully and joyfully on stringed instruments. (Psalm 33:1–3, GW)

DAY 202

Fresh Manna

One day I woke up at 4:00 am, and I wasn't ready to be awake. I was tired and annoyed and just wanted to go back to sleep—but instead, a thought captured my attention. The thought was "fresh manna from heaven." God provided manna to the Israelites every morning. It remained fresh as long as they ate it that day, but if they tried to keep it overnight, it became rotten.

We need to be living on fresh revelation from the Word of God—we can't live on yesterday's food. Jesus is the bread of life—our manna from heaven—so partake of Him each morning.

> *Do not work for food that spoils, but for food that endures to eternal life, which the Son of Man will give you. For on him God the Father has placed his seal of approval....*
>
> *Then Jesus declared, "I am the bread of life. Whoever comes to me will never go hungry, and whoever believes in me will never be thirsty."* (John 6:27, 35, NIV)

DAY 203

A Place of Confinement

God sometimes speaks to us when we are least expecting it, as He did to me when He gave me a word about John the Revelator. John was exiled to the island of Patmos because of his faithful witness for Jesus. The authorities thought this would silence him, but Jesus can't be silenced. Not then and not now! Nothing can stop His Word from going forth.

On Patmos, during John's time of greatest confinement, he received a prophetic revelation of what was to come. Just like a woman in labour, his confinement gave birth to the book of Revelation. John couldn't be silenced, because God was with Him.

The enemy will try to exile our faith—to quiet us and cause us to quit. Discouragement enters through difficult situations, but if we just keep praising God, the devil can't stop us or silence us. Faith has a sound! You may feel like you are all alone or imprisoned, or that circumstances have rendered you incapable, but that isn't so. Get ready for God to birth something through you. If you will let God, He wants to use you—and all of His servants—to speak forth what He is saying. We all have a voice to witness, teach, preach, write songs and books, prophesy, and flow in the gifts of the Spirit.

> *I was exiled to the island of Patmos for preaching the Word of God and for my testimony about Jesus. It was the Lord's Day, and I was worshiping in the Spirit. Suddenly, I heard behind me a loud voice like a trumpet blast. It said, "Write in a book everything you see..."*
> (Revelation 1:9b–11a, NLT)

DAY 204

Be a God-Seeker

When we read the Bible in several different translations, it gives us a fuller picture of what is being said.

I will bless the Lord at all times; his praise shall continually be in my mouth. (Psalm 34:1, ESV)

I will glory in the Lord; let the afflicted hear and rejoice. Glorify the Lord with me; let us exalt his name together. I sought the Lord, and he answered me; he delivered me from all my fears. (Psalm 34:2–4, NIV)

Those who look to him for help will be radiant with joy; no shadow of shame will darken their faces. In my desperation I prayed, and the Lord listened; he saved me from all my troubles. For the angel of the Lord is a guard; he surrounds and defends all who fear him.
Taste and see that the Lord is good. Oh, the joys of those who take refuge in him! Fear the Lord, you his godly people, for those who fear him will have all they need. Even strong young lions sometimes go hungry, but those who trust in the Lord will lack no good thing. (Psalm 34:5–10, NLT)

The Lord is near the brokenhearted; he delivers those who are discouraged. The godly face many dangers, but the Lord saves them from each one of them. (Psalm 34:18–19, NET)

Psalm 34 talks about praising, seeking, and trusting God, and the joy of deliverance that comes from being a God-seeker. All we need to do is seek and trust in the Lord, keeping our eyes fixed on Him. We can count on God; He is our solid rock, so there is no need to worry about tomorrow.

DAY 205

Blinded by the Truth

One evening I was praying about ISIS. I began to pray against the spirits behind that organization. The real enemy is not the people, because they are blinded to truth. Those who are part of these terrorist groups are in great darkness—they are deceived. As Christians, we have a responsibility to love our enemies and pray for them.

> *For we do not wrestle against flesh and blood, but against principalities, against powers, against the rulers of the darkness of this age, against spiritual hosts of wickedness in the heavenly places.* (Ephesians 6:12, NKJV)

If we hate, we are no better than them. Having a reason doesn't give us the right to hate. It's awful that Christians are being martyred, but they are now experiencing the reality of eternal life, whereas the murderers are headed for eternal death. Paul persecuted and killed Christians, thinking he was right. We need to pray for a supernatural encounter with Jesus for these terrorists, just like Paul's road to Damascus experience.

> *But I say to you, love your enemies, bless those who curse you, do good to those who hate you, and pray for those who spitefully use you and persecute you.* (Matthew 5:44, NKJV)

> *Then Jesus said, "Father, forgive them, for they do not know what they do."* (Luke 23:34a, NKJV)

DAY 206

His Grace Is All We Need

I was reminded once again of God's overwhelming grace, which helps us to release and lay things aside. It may not be that we don't want to let go of the past—perhaps we are just comfortable where we are. A baby bird is comfortable in its nest, but it must learn to fly. We can soar into our new season if we keep in mind that change is progressive—a continual forward motion.

> *He said to me, "My grace is enough for you, because power is made perfect in weakness." So I'll gladly spend my time bragging about my weaknesses so that Christ's power can rest on me. Therefore, I'm all right with weaknesses, insults, disasters, harassments, and stressful situations for the sake of Christ, because when I'm weak, then I'm strong.* (2 Corinthians 12:9–10, CEB)

DAY 207

God's Grace Surrounds Us

God's grace surrounds us like a shield! With His grace, we can weather any storm, any fire, and any flood. His grace surrounds us. God is with us always—He is our redeemer!

> *But now, says the Lord—the one who created you, Jacob, the one who formed you, Israel: Don't fear, for I have redeemed you; I have called you by name; you are mine. When you pass through the waters, I will be with you; when through the rivers, they won't sweep over you. When you walk through the fire, you won't be scorched and flame won't burn you....*
>
> *You are my witnesses, says the Lord, my servant, whom I chose, so that you would know and believe me and understand that I am the one. Before me no god was formed; after me there has been no other.... From the dawn of time, I am the one. No one can escape my power. I act, and who can undo it?...*
>
> *Don't remember the prior things; don't ponder ancient history. Look! I'm doing a new thing; now it sprouts up; don't you recognize it? I'm making a way in the desert, paths in the wilderness. ...I have put water in the desert and streams in the wilderness to give water to my people, my chosen ones...* (Isaiah 43:1–2, 10, 13, 18–19, 20b, CEB)

DAY 208

Put Your Trust in Me

One day as I was praying for someone who was facing a difficult situation, a thought came to me: "Faith operates in an atmosphere of peace." If we are experiencing fear, worry, or anxiety, our faith will be hindered. God is in control, no matter what else may be happening. Our hope stands firm because of Jesus' blood and righteousness. Let it be said of me that in every circumstance my hope—my strength—is in Christ alone!

> *But I will bless the person who puts his trust in me.* (Jeremiah 17:7, GNT)

DAY 209

Wildfire from Heaven

At a praise night in my church, I had a thought about "wildfire from heaven," and pictured lightning coming from the very hands of the Lord and striking people. Having grown up in Western Canada, my parents had friends who worked for BC Forestry, and they often shared detailed information regarding forest fires. Carelessness caused some conflagrations, but lightning was the number one reason for the majority of forest fires. Controlled burns are started purposely to clean up dead debris, but wildfires are very difficult to put out. They burn up everything in their path, and they change direction with the wind, making them very difficult to extinguish.

The Lord is sending His light, power, glory, and presence as lightning, and His lightning is going to start wildfires in individual people, churches, and regions. It will burn out of control in all directions, fanned by the winds of the Holy Spirit. This is a fire that cannot be contained, burning and catching everything in its path on fire. Some of us may have been on fire in the past, but the fire seems like it has gone out. However, it's still smouldering inside of us, and it's about to be reignited by lightning from heaven.

> *The Lord is King! Let the earth rejoice!... Fire spreads ahead of him and burns up all his foes. His lightning flashes out across the world. The earth sees and trembles. The mountains melt like wax before the Lord, before the Lord of all the earth.* (Psalm 97:1a, 3–5, NLT)

This holy fire from heaven is going to consume everything, melting every mountain and obstacle that stands in our way. Thank God for wildfire from heaven!

DAY 210

The Holy Spirit and Fire

The Lord showed me a picture at the beginning of this year of a black torch shaped like the Olympic torch, but with fireworks instead of flames. The fireworks streamed out and flowed in different directions. During prayer, God showed me that we are the black torch and the fire is burning up everything hindering and holding us back. After it's gone, God will release a fountain of fire flowing out of us in all directions. The fire coming from the torch is meant to start a wildfire in those who have never burned, and re-ignite those whose fire is smouldering and needing to be rekindled once again. It's time to be filled with wildfire from heaven!

> *I baptize you with water to show that you have repented, but the one who will come after me will baptize you with the Holy Spirit and fire.* (Matthew 3:11a, GNT)

DAY 211
An All-Consuming Fire

I see what God showed me about lightning coming from heaven in everything I read and hear. My pastor was preaching about coming to the altar and getting into God's presence, and I wrote a thought down: "If we want the fire of God, we need to build an altar to God." When we lay ourselves on that altar as a sacrifice, the fire of God will consume us.

God is an all-consuming fire. He wants us to burn for Him, but just like the burning bush, we won't burn up or burn out. We become a wildfire that cannot be stopped or put out as His lightning storm sets us on fire. I see His light, power, and glory, consuming His people as we press into His presence and lay ourselves on His altar. Then I see us going out with resurrection power.

For the Lord your God is a consuming fire, a jealous God. (Deuteronomy 4:24, NKJV)

For our God is a consuming fire. (Hebrews 12:29, NKJV)

DAY 212

Set Us on Fire

I looked up some information on wildfires recently, and discovered that a wildfire starts most easily when the conditions are very dry, such as lightning striking a very dry tree. A lightning strike is a massive electrical charge between the atmosphere and an earthbound object, causing an uncontrolled fire that is fuelled by the wind and spreading in all directions—even jumping over roads and rivers.

Spiritually, there are some very dry people, churches, and regions. An atmosphere electrified with the lightning of God coming from His very throne will strike us earthbound objects and start a wildfire in us. If we allow it to spread to those around us, it will burn up everything in its path, jumping over hindrances and obstacles, fuelled by the winds of the Holy Spirit. Everything dead and dry in our lives will burn away and bring forth new growth. Let this massive electrical charge from heaven strike a wildfire in you!

He covers His hands with lightning, And commands it to strike. (Job 36:32, NKJV)

DAY 213
A Fire that Can't Be Put Out

We aren't ever supposed to bury a campfire, as it will continue to smoulder and catch roots on fire, eventually reaching the surface and starting a wildfire.

For many Christians, our roots go deep in our relationship with God. We have experienced His fire in our lives, but we may think it has gone out. However, it's just buried deep inside, and it's still smouldering. It may have only been a small fire in the past, but it's resurfacing—and this time it's going be a raging inferno!

An underground fire is fed combustible vegetation. If we will keep going back into God's presence no matter how dry we feel, we are creating the right environment for the fire within us to flare up. For those who have never experienced the fire of God, the lightning of God is going to start a wildfire in their dry and parched lives. This scripture describes a natural forest fire, but it can be compared to what the Lord is saying to us, the Body of Christ:

> *Tell the southern forest to hear what the Sovereign Lord is saying: Look! I am starting a fire, and it will burn up every tree in you, whether green or dry. Nothing will be able to put it out. It will spread from south to north, and everyone will feel the heat of the flames.* (Ezekiel 20:47, GNT)

DAY 214

Lord Over the Whole Earth

It's absolutely essential that we place our trust and confidence in the Lord, so we can show forth His power and might to the nations of this earth. They have been deceived into worshipping false gods. We need the fire of God to set us ablaze, because we want all to know that Jesus is Lord over the whole earth.

> *Lord, you are the one who protects me and gives me strength; you help me in times of trouble. Nations will come to you from the ends of the earth and say, "Our ancestors had nothing but false gods, nothing but useless idols. Can people make their own gods? No, if they did, those would not really be gods."*
>
> *"So then," says the Lord, "once and for all I will make the nations know my power and my might; they will know that I am the Lord."* (Jeremiah 16:19–21, GNT)

DAY 215

The Centrepiece

The Lord is the centrepiece of our lives, and the one we give our attention to. A table that is set very beautifully is wonderful to look at, but the centrepiece is what draws everyone's attention. Our eyes are drawn to the centrepiece first.

At a wedding, the beautiful bridesmaids and maid of honour lead the procession. The groom watches them, but is looking in anticipation for the bride to enter the room. When the bride walks in, all eyes are fixed on her because she is the centrepiece, the focus of everyone's attention.

Praise draws us into God's presence, where we can set our focus on Him. He needs to be the centre of our lives—the one we give our full attention to. When looking at the life of Peter in the Bible we tend to see the negative first and not the amazing life of faith he led. Peter did take his eyes off the Lord, and began to sink because he looked at the size of the waves on the sea. We have the tendency to look at circumstances too, causing us to be overtaken by the storms of life. But just as the Lord showed with Peter, He is always there to lend a helping hand, and that helps us to refocus. If we keep looking to Him, we won't sink or stay off course for long.

Peter may have taken his eyes momentarily off Jesus, but he had the courage to do what no one else did. He stepped into the unknown when He stepped out onto the water. Peter may have had little faith, but he still had more than the others. The other disciples stayed where they felt safe, in a place of comfort. Our faith may be the size of a mustard seed, but it's enough to take the next step. We often allow our comfort level to determine how we communicate in worship, but we need to have the courage to step into unfamiliar expressions. Let's keep our focus on Jesus, allowing Him to take us into the new and unknown.

But you are a chosen people, a royal priesthood, a holy nation, God's special possession, that you may declare the praises of him who called you out of darkness into his wonderful light. (1 Peter 2:9, NIV)

Dick Eastman writes in his book *Intercessory Worship: Combining Worship & Prayer to Touch the Heart of God*, "Worship enthrones God. Worship provides a place for God to dwell on earth in all his fullness."[3] The Lord is the centrepiece of all worship when we keep our full attention on Him!

DAY 216

The Way into His Presence

There is no distance between us and the Lord, our King and our God, but we need to learn how to gain access to Him. Queen Esther lived in the palace as the wife of the king, but she had no access to him unless he called for her. A grave situation arose for her people and she needed to gain entrance to the king immediately to obtain his favour. Esther made a choice to fast and pray, and instructed all her people to do the same. In doing so, Esther found favour with the king and was able to save her people. We learn from the story of Esther to trust that God's favour will be extended to us as we approach Him in joyful praise and worship.

> *Shout out praises to the Lord, all the earth! Worship the Lord with joy! Enter his presence with joyful singing! Acknowledge that the Lord is God! He made us and we belong to him; we are his people, the sheep of his pasture. Enter his gates with thanksgiving, and his courts with praise! Give him thanks! Praise his name! For the Lord is good. His loyal love endures, and he is faithful through all generations.* (Psalm 100, NET)

DAY 217

Don't Stay Stuck in the Mud

My life was radically altered in a matter of seconds, and I had no choice but to immediately embrace a new season. Things can happen outside of our control to cause life-altering change, so we must accept, embrace, and go with it.

However, sometimes we can be moving forward when we seem to find ourselves in a rut: we can't go back, but we aren't able to move forward either. When a car is stuck, the tires are spinning but going nowhere. Sometimes we just need a little push from behind while we press on the gas.

Pressing into God gives you the fuel to get unstuck. We all need someone to encourage us to move forward, but we must do our part as well. When we join with others who also want change, it is actually much easier to accomplish. Think of the four friends of the paralyzed man who climbed a house while carrying him on his bed, and then ripped a hole in the roof so they could lower him in front of Jesus for healing. A true friend will always push and encourage you towards God's presence. We won't stay stuck in a paralyzed position if we come to Jesus.

Are you tired? Worn out? Burned out on religion? Come to me. Get away with me and you'll recover your life. I'll show you how to take a real rest. Walk with me and work with me—watch how I do it. Learn the unforced rhythms of grace. (Matthew 11:28–29, MSG)

DAY 218

Burn in Us

I woke up one morning with these words on my heart, so I wrote them down. This ought to be our hearts' cry—that once again, God would baptize us with the Holy Spirit and fire!

Let your fire burn so bright, consuming the darkness and the night. Filling us with your power and might! Burn in us for the whole world to see. Burn in you and me. I see lightning, Father, flowing from your hands, hitting the mark, it only takes a spark to light us on fire with your Holy Spirit and fire! Burn in us for the whole world to see. Burn in you and burn in me. Light up this parched land with flames of love from your hand. Wildfire from heaven that can't be put out! Let us shout it out. This is my prayer: Burn in us, burn in us, burn in us for the world to see. Burn in you, and burn in me. Let this be our hearts' cry: set us on fire that we may burn for all the world to see.

Let your light so shine before men, that they may see your good works and glorify your Father in heaven. (Matthew 5:16, NKJV)

DAY 219

He Is Always Ready to Help

God is always good to us, His people. He always comes through for us, and His love is everlasting. No matter the situation, God is there and ready to help. All we need to do is ask and He will respond to us—every time.

> *Shout praises to the Lord! He is good to us, and his love never fails. Everyone the Lord has rescued from trouble should praise him, everyone he has brought from the east and the west, the north and the south....*
>
> *You were hungry and thirsty and about to give up. You were in serious trouble, but you prayed to the Lord, and he rescued you....*
>
> *You should praise the Lord for his love and for the wonderful things he does for all of us. To everyone who is thirsty, he gives something to drink; to everyone who is hungry, he gives good things to eat.*
>
> *Some of you were prisoners suffering in deepest darkness and bound by chains....*
>
> *You were in serious trouble, but you prayed to the Lord, and he rescued you. He brought you out of the deepest darkness and broke your chains.*
>
> *You should praise the Lord for his love and for the wonderful things he does for all of us* (Psalm 107:1–3, 5–6, 8–10, 13–15, CEV)

Nothing will encourage us like pressing into God's presence with joyful praise and worship. King David was a man after God's own heart—a prayer warrior and a worshipper of God. We learn from the life of David to encourage ourselves in the Lord and to praise God in every situation, knowing that nothing can prevent us from receiving total victory. He will answer you and come to your rescue every time.

> *But, Lord, you are my shield, my wonderful God who gives me courage. I will pray to the Lord, and he will answer me from his holy mountain.* (Psalm 3:3–4, NCV)

DAY 220

Don't Let the Light of Christ Go Out

We used to experience power outages quite often when we lived on our acreage. Those outages made us more appreciative and aware of how essential water and power are to our lives. In a spiritual context, without the power of the Holy Spirit we find ourselves living in the dark, and eventually we will grow cold and dry.

We can do nothing about a natural power outage except for wait for someone to fix it, but we can make sure we don't let the Light of Christ—His power—go out in our lives. Don't let the well run dry; keep the water of His Spirit flowing in your life.

But you shall receive power when the Holy Spirit has come upon you; and you shall be witnesses to Me in Jerusalem, and in all Judea and Samaria, and to the end of the earth. (Acts 1:8, NKJV)

If anyone thirsts, let him come to Me and drink. He who believes in Me, as the Scripture has said, out of his heart will flow rivers of living water. (John 7:37b–38, NKJV)

DAY 221

Cleanse and Purify

We can learn a lot from the natural things we do in life. A cleanse removes the toxins and impurities from your body that aren't supposed to be there. Although you may feel worse momentarily, once your body has been cleansed you will feel much more energetic and less sluggish than before. That is what pressing into God's presence will do for you!

If you are tired, weary, overwhelmed, discouraged, oppressed, fearful, angry, unforgiving, bitter, or burdened by the cares of life, you need to rid your spirit of those things. They are toxic to your life. When we press into God's presence over and over, we will be cleansed and purified. His fire will burn away our impurities, and his rain will refresh us. The wind of His Spirit will blow away things that weary us. Come to God and let Him cleanse you from all unrighteousness, from everything that holds you back. It's something we need to do daily.

> *Are you tired? Worn out? Burned out on religion? Come to me. Get away with me and you will recover your life. I'll show you how to take a real rest. Walk with me and work with me—watch how I do it. Learn the unforced rhythms of grace. I won't lay anything heavy or ill-fitting on you. Keep company with me and you'll learn to live freely and lightly.* (Matthew 11:28–30, MSG)

DAY 222

It's Time to Clean House

One day as I was going through things in anticipation of moving to a different house, I threw and gave away several bags of stuff. It was amazing—I had thought it was all so useful or necessary enough to keep stored away. It's totally mind-boggling what we collect over time—and I still had another closet and storage room to go through.

It makes me think about the junk we have stored up in our hearts: past hurts, unforgiveness, envy, and bad memories. I have never seen myself as a hoarder, but I think I'm more of one than I had realized.

A move causes us to get rid of things that need to go. It's amazing how good we feel when we get rid of stuff we don't need. I'm sure we all have things safely packed away in our heart, but we can't keep them hidden forever. What are we hoarding in our hearts? It's time for a housecleaning! It's time to release the secret things of our heart that hinder us from moving forward in God. If it's cluttering your life, just throw it away!

For everything that is hidden will eventually be brought into the open, and every secret will be brought to light. (Mark 4:22, NLT)

For all that is secret will eventually be brought into the open, and everything that is concealed will be brought to light and made known to all. (Luke 8:17, NLT)

DAY 223

An Extravaganza of Praise

The Holy Spirit stirs up our spirit, and for me, sometimes it's like a volcano that's about to erupt inside. I was thinking about King David and how he loved to worship God. He wasn't quiet in his worship: he was loud, expressive, and passionate. While meditating on this, a thought came to me, "It's time for the people of God to show forth an extravaganza of praise," and I wondered what that was.

An extravaganza of praise is radical, passion-filled worship clothed in the zeal of God. Can you imagine what that would look like? The word "extravaganza" in the Merriam-Webster dictionary means "a literary or musical work marked by extreme freedom of style and structure… a lavish or spectacular show or event."[4] Urbandictionary.com defines it as "anything fun that usually involves something you haven't done before with the most fun friends you know."[5]

It's time to show forth the praises of God passionately in enjoyable new ways with the most fun friends you know. Let's lift songs to God with extreme freedom of expression in musical style and structure, just like King David did when he danced before the Lord with great zeal. It's time for an exuberant eruption—an extravaganza of praise to God!

> *But the righteous are glad; they rejoice before God and celebrate with joy.* (Psalm 68:3, HCSB)

> *Sing praises to God and to his name! Sing loud praises to him who rides the clouds. His name is the Lord—rejoice in his presence!* (Psalm 68:4, NLT)

Shout with joy to the Lord, all the earth; burst into songs and make music. Make music to the Lord with harps, with harps and the sound of singing. (Psalm 98:4–5, NCV)

DAY 224

Let It Grow

We all go through trials and storms—that's life! How we react to them is what makes all the difference. As we share with others what we have learned through the difficulties we've faced, it will encourage them to weather the storms that undoubtedly will arise in their lives. We can use the things that have happened to us, both positive and negative, to help us grow and mature as believers in Christ, better enabling us to be a blessing to others.

> *Dear brothers and sisters, when troubles of any kind come your way, consider it an opportunity for great joy. For you know that when your faith is tested, your endurance has a chance to grow. So let it grow, for when your endurance is fully developed, you will be perfect and complete, needing nothing.* (James 1:2–4, NLT)

DAY 225

Oh, How He Loves Us So

There are times in our lives when the Lord says something and it stops us in our tracks, making us question, "Is that really what I heard?" We know that we are valuable and precious to the Lord—but do we truly believe it?

One day as I was driving and praising God, I heard Him say to me, "Do you know you are My everything?"

I wondered if I'd heard right. I said to God, "Yes, You are my everything," and He replied very clearly "No—I said, do you know you are My everything?"

I asked God again, "How can I be Your everything?"

Once more He said, "You are My everything: everything I came to the earth for, everything I went to the cross for, everything I suffered for, everything I shed my blood and died for. Everything I defeated hell for, everything I rose from the dead for, everything I am coming back for—you are my everything!"

Praise the Lord—we are everything to Him! Oh, how He loves us so!

For God so loved the world that He gave His only begotten Son, that whoever believes in Him should not perish but have everlasting life. (John 3:16, NKJV)

DAY 226

Temples of Praise

One of the greatest examples of worship took place at David's temple during a time in history when the tent was open for all to see and the ark was not veiled. The Israelites worshipped freely in His presence.

Dick Eastman writes in his book *Intercessory Worship*, "Worship at David's tent was open, and David's kingdom was vastly multiplied as a result. Cultivating a climate of open worship, I believe, will help hasten the restoration of David's fallen tent and soften hearts for history's greatest harvest."[6]

Each of us is a temple of praise. When we praise with our whole hearts, lifting the Name of Jesus, hearts will be softened and many will be drawn to the Lord. God will restore His people to be a people of praise.

> *In that day I will restore the fallen house of David. I will repair its damaged walls. From the ruins I will rebuild it and restore its former glory.* (Amos 9:11, NLT)

DAY 227

Worship Is Eternal

Worship is eternal—it will never end. We need to learn how to cultivate a lifestyle of worship now in preparation for eternity, when we will be worshipping the Lord forever.

> *I will bless the Lord at all times; His praise shall continually be in my mouth.* (Psalm 34:1, NKJV)

I love what this radical seventeenth-century monk, Brother Lawrence, said to his fellow monks on his deathbed: "I am not dying; I'm just doing what I have been doing for the past forty years, and doing what I expect to be doing for all eternity."

"What is that?" a monk asked.

Brother Lawrence answered, "I am worshipping the God I love!"

> *I will extol You, my God, O King; And I will bless Your name forever and ever. Every day I will bless You, and I will praise Your name forever and ever.* (Psalm 145:1–2, NKJV)

DAY 228

Breakthrough

One evening I was driving home and thinking about the tough season I had found myself in. It was difficult, but at the same time exciting. There were great trials, but also huge victories. It was a breakthrough year in which I stepped out and did some things that I'd dreamed about and held in my heart for many years.

The more we are willing to step up to the plate and do what the Lord puts on our hearts, the bolder we will become. Then when the Lord has something for us to share, we'll be more confident to speak out. We need to stop being afraid to make a mistake. In the middle of one of my biggest breakthroughs came by far my greatest trial.

We need to keep running to the Lord—no matter what's going on. Then, we'll break through the darkness into a place of great joy and peace, and the walls in our lives that have held us back will crumble. Like a sea wall along an ocean, the barrier stops the waves from breaking through, but without it, there is nothing that can stop the water.

Do not remember the former things, Nor consider the things of old. Behold, I will do a new thing, Now it shall spring forth; Shall you not know it? I will even make a road in the wilderness and rivers in the desert. (Isaiah 43:18–19, NKJV)

DAY 229

The Sound of My People Rising

I woke up suddenly one night because I heard an audible sound coming from inside me. It wasn't coming from my mouth—it was an internal sound, and I could feel it in my chest. It sounded like a horn or shofar, and I know that sound because I've heard it in both Israel and Indonesia. The sound didn't last long, but it had a big impact on me. This is what came to me: "It's the sound of My Spirit rising from within My people. It starts within, and then it will be heard without."

The Lord reminded me of my first night in Indonesia. My daughter Breanna and I were staying in a guesthouse north of Jakarta in a city called Bandung. I was tired after a long trip, but was finding it hard to sleep as our days and nights were switched around. It was early morning when I heard the mournful call to prayer, and I complained to the Lord, saying, "I don't like that sound—I just want to sleep." While I was complaining, the Lord reminded me of a Bible verse:

> *Arise, shine; For your light has come! And the glory of the Lord is risen upon you. For behold, the darkness shall cover the earth, And deep darkness the people; But the Lord will arise over you, And His glory will be seen upon you.* (Isaiah 60:1–2, NKJV)

His Spirit is rising within us with a sound that is about to be released, resulting in the greatest harvest in the history of mankind. God's people are being called to arise by a joyful sound flowing from their spirit.

DAY 230

A Sound from Within

God impressed upon me that the audible sound I heard in the night was the sound of His people rising. The story of Jericho came to mind because of the impact of the sound that rose from the Israelites and gave them victory.

The people of God walked in silence around the city for seven days, and then seven times on the last day. They may have been silent on the outside, but a sound was rising on the inside. When the horn was blown and Joshua said, "Shout—I have given you the city!" they shouted and the walls came down. That same sound of victory is rising from within us—let's shout for the salvation of our city!

> *Now Joshua had commanded the people, saying, "You shall not shout or make any noise with your voice, nor shall a word proceed out of your mouth, until the day I say to you, 'Shout!' Then you shall shout!" ...Joshua said to the people: "Shout, for the Lord has given you the city!"* (Joshua 6:10, 16b, NKJV)

DAY 231

Follow Hard After God

We need to learn to be in continual pursuit of God. King David is a great example to us—he was a man of prayer and a worshipper of God. He was a man who followed hard after God. David was far from perfect, but he knew where to run when in trouble. He knew his help came from the maker of heaven and earth. David was a true worshipper of God—he would play his harp and sing, causing the spirits tormenting King Saul to leave. Worship will send demonic spirits fleeing, as they can't stay where the presence of God abides.

> *I praise you, Lord, for answering my prayers. You are my strong shield, and I trust you completely. You have helped me, and I will celebrate and thank you in song.*
>
> *You give strength to your people, Lord, and you save and protect your chosen ones. Come save us and bless us. Be our shepherd and always carry us in your arms.* (Psalm 28:6–9, CEV)

DAY 232

His Voice Will Be Heard

There is a sound rising in God's people; the volume is increasing, and His voice will be heard through us. John was exiled to the island of Patmos in an attempt by the enemy to silence him. His foes thought they could shut John up by confining him, but they just set him up to write the Book of Revelation. He was in the Spirit on the Lord's Day and as he chose to worship, God birthed something through him.

The enemy tried to silence Paul and Silas as well by throwing them into prison, but their place of confinement also became a place of birthing. As they sang and rejoiced loudly, freedom came to them and all the other prisoners—including the jailer and his whole household. Their enemies had tried to stop them from preaching by imprisoning them. They thought it would silence their voices, but as Paul and Silas praised, the very foundation of the prison was shaken, causing chains to fall off and doors to be opened.

Our voices will bring freedom to our own lives and those of others. They will shake the very foundations of those things in our lives that keep us imprisoned, and remove the chains that keep us bound. Doors will open and set us free, resulting in harvest, just as it happened with Paul and Silas.

> *But at midnight Paul and Silas were praying and singing hymns to God, and the prisoners were listening to them. Suddenly there was a great earthquake, so that the foundations of the prison were shaken; and immediately all the doors were opened and everyone's chains were loosed....*
>
> *And he [the jailer] brought them out and said, "Sirs, what must I do to be saved?"* (Acts 16:25–26, 30, NKJV)

DAY 233

Praise Is the Antidote

Life can seem overwhelming at times, so we must learn to rejoice and be thankful in all situations by encouraging ourselves in the Lord. There isn't anything that can stop us: no mountain, valley, desert, or storm we can't get through when we put our trust in the God of all hope!

Praise is the antidote for depression, hopelessness, fear, anxiety, and any other negative thoughts or feelings. The Psalms show David's example of how to make it through life's difficulties. Have you ever been depressed, overwhelmed, or hopeless, feeling like darkness was closing in? David did, and this Psalm was his response. Let it be yours!

Listen, Lord, as I pray! You are faithful and honest and will answer my prayer.... My enemies are chasing me, crushing me in the ground.... I have given up all hope, and I feel numb all over.

I remember to think about the many things you did in years gone by. Then I lift my hands in prayer, because my soul is a desert, thirsty for water from you.

Please hurry, Lord, and answer my prayer. I feel hopeless....

Each morning let me learn more about your love because I trust you. I come to you in prayer, asking for your guidance.

Please rescue me from my enemies, Lord! I come to you for safety. You are my God. Show me what you want me to do, and let your gentle Spirit lead me in the right path.

Be true to your name, Lord, and keep my life safe. Use your saving power to protect me from trouble. I am your servant. Show

how much you love me by destroying my enemies. (Psalm 143:1, 3a, 4–7a, 8–12, CEV)

Rejoice in Him every day, choosing to bless the Lord, and His joy will become your strength.

DAY 234

The Name of the Lord Shall Be Praised

Hallelujah! You servants of the Lord, praise him. Praise the name of the Lord. Thank the name of the Lord now and forever. From where the sun rises to where the sun sets, the name of the Lord should be praised. The Lord is high above all the nations. His glory is above the heavens. Who is like the Lord our God? He is seated on his high throne. He bends down to look at heaven and earth. He lifts the poor from the dust. He lifts the needy from a garbage heap. He seats them with influential people, with the influential leaders of his people. He makes a woman who is in a childless home a joyful mother. Hallelujah! (Psalm 113, GW)

He is deserving of our praise all day, every day! Praise should go forth from the Lord's people around the clock—sundown to sunup. The Lord showed me this a few years ago. In a vision, a small group of us were praying and kneeling on the floor, and the sun was going down, rising up, and then going down again as we were praying. The sun went up and down over a map of the world in a circular motion.

The nations of this world need to be covered with worship and prayer all day, every day. The enemy is working 24/7 to destroy people, so we need to pray continually to see people set free and saved. Worship and intercession will change the atmosphere over cities, regions, and nations. They will send the enemy fleeing and bring in the harvest, but we have to battle in the Spirit. It won't happen by casual prayer—rather by zealous, intense, continual worship to our God.

> *Rejoice always, pray without ceasing...* (1 Thessalonians 5:16–17, NKJV)

DAY 235

Being Thankful Always Leads to Rejoicing

Being thankful will always lead to rejoicing. We all have much to be thankful for. When difficulties come our way, it is always an opportunity for us to look and see the good in life and be thankful. If we will learn to give thanks to the Lord no matter what life throws our way, we will always react by rejoicing. This doesn't mean that what we're going through isn't extremely difficult, but we rejoice in knowing that God is always good and merciful.

Nobody went through anything more difficult than Jesus, but He endured for the joy that He knew would come by His obedience—even unto death on the cross. Paul went through many difficulties: beatings, stoning, being left for dead, being shipwrecked, persecution, and imprisonment. But look how he reacted—he was thankful, and he rejoiced. Paul and Silas' experience in jail is a great example of this.

> *Rejoice always, pray continually, give thanks in all circumstances; for this is God's will for you in Christ Jesus.* (1 Thessalonians 5:16–18, NIV)

When I was told the shocking news that my husband had passed away, the first thing the Lord told me was to rejoice. That isn't an easy thing to do in such circumstances, but I knew that I had to obey what God said. At the time I was in Kenya on a mission trip with my friend Pat. I told her what the Lord had said, and all the way back home we listened to music, rejoiced, and prayed. The more we continued to rejoice, the more there seemed to be to rejoice about. Worshipping the

Lord takes the focus off oneself and puts it on God! I knew that my husband was in heaven, and that in itself was enough reason to rejoice and be thankful.

Rejoicing with a thankful heart truly does bring freedom. I was set free from the fear of the future and of being alone. I was set free from self-pity, anger, unforgiveness, and grief overtaking my life. It only made me stronger, bolder, freer, and more determined to make my life count and to help others find freedom from the enemy's grip.

Whenever you find yourselves in a tough situation, count it all joy and be thankful, knowing that no matter what happens in life, we will win—because Jesus already has!

I have given you the authority to trample snakes and scorpions and to destroy the enemy's power. Nothing will hurt you. However, don't be happy that evil spirits obey you. Be happy that your names are written in heaven. (Luke 10:19–20, GW)

DAY 236
In the Time of the Harvest

The story of the Israelites crossing the Jordan River is a story of faith. It was a step of faith and obedience as the priests stepped into the water.

> ...and the feet of the priests who bore the ark dipped in the edge of the water (for the Jordan overflows all its banks during the whole time of harvest)... (Joshua 3:15b, NKJV)

It is harvest time, and as we step out in faith and obedience, we will see an overflow of His presence in our lives individually and corporately. The priests walked right into the miraculous as they stepped into the water in obedience, and so will we if we obey. God wants to do wonders among us, just as He did for the Israelites. He wants us to enter the Promised Land, but just as the Israelites didn't possess it without a fight, neither will we. They had to go to war even though it was the time of harvest. They still had to fight battles for it, starting with Jericho.

The land represents the souls of people, and we are going to have to battle for them. The Israelites fought a physical battle, but ours is a spiritual one. As we step out in faith during harvest time, God will deliver us—whether by holding the enemy back so we advance, or causing walls to fall. How God chooses to deliver us is up to Him—our part is to step out and believe.

> The horse is prepared for the day of battle, But deliverance is of the Lord. (Proverbs 21:31, NKJV)

DAY 237

Follow the Ark

The story of the Israelites crossing the Jordan River is encouraging. The people were to follow the priests, who were the only ones allowed to carry the ark that housed the presence of God. The Bible calls us a royal priesthood, and we are carriers of His presence. The Israelites had never been that way before, so they were told to keep their eyes on the ark. The presence of God was with the priests as they stepped into Jordan River.

Under the new covenant, as priests we carry God's presence. So when our High Priest Jesus commands us to step into the water, we need to do it. We need to make a channel by faith for people so they can get past all the obstacles blocking the way to their Promised Land. When we do this, God will make a way, even where there seems to be no way.

> *Proclaim this among the nations: Prepare for war! ...Let the weak say, "I am strong."*
>
> *Put in the sickle, for the harvest is ripe. Come, go down; for the winepress is full...*
>
> *The Lord also will roar from Zion...* (Joel 3:9a, 10b, 13a, 16a, NKJV)

It's time for His presence to overflow from us to others, as this passage from the book of Joel declares when it describes the winepress being full. Just like in the story of the Israelites crossing the Jordan, the river of God is at a flood stage in our lives. We need to go forward with a shout prepared for battle, influencing those in the valley of decision to make a choice for Christ. As we praise, shout, and lift the Name of Jesus, walls will come down in people's lives, drawing them to the Lord by the Holy Spirit. It's time to reap—the harvest is ready!

DAY 238

One Purpose, One Goal, and One Sound

It's important for the body of Christ that we unite as churches, with the goal of encouraging and building one another up so we can take our cities, provinces, and nation for the Lord. This can only be accomplished by joining together in worship, prayer, preaching of the Word, and fellowship. The walls of Jericho fell because of the united marching and shouting of the Israelites. The sound of unity shook the city to its foundations and its walls fell down, giving the Israelites victory.

> *The priests blew the trumpets.*
> *When the people heard the blast of the trumpets, they gave a thunderclap shout. The wall fell at once. The people rushed straight into the city and took it.* (Joshua 6:20, MSG)

DAY 239

You Have a Destiny Planned by God

In two chapters of Jeremiah, 1 and 29, God tells us that He knows us and has a destiny planned for us. God knows all the good things, trials, and difficulties we will encounter—long before they ever happen. When the storms of life come, we can ride the waves without drowning because God always prepares in advance. If we allow those things to grow and mature us, they can push us into the destiny that was planned for us before we ever existed.

Just press into God's presence and you will step into His river of destiny. It will take you into your Promised Land. Trials of life are just the battles and obstacles we have to overcome to reach our destiny.

> *For the Lord your God is bringing you into a good land of flowing streams and pools of water, with fountains and springs that gush out in the valleys and hills.* (Deuteronomy 8:7, NLT)

DAY 240

Commanded to Love

I woke up singing the chorus from the song "One Thing Remains" composed by Jeremy Riddle and Brian Johnson. It talks about how God's love is unfailing. His love will always remain.

Love is more than a feeling—it is a command from God. We need to choose every day to allow the love of God to flow out of our hearts by the Holy Spirit. I was reminded of the time when the Lord told me that I was His everything, and I responded that He was everything to me. Each of us is everything to God! We are everything Jesus died and rose again for, and everything He is coming back for. We are everything to the Lord. Oh, how He loves us so!

For God so loved the world that He gave His only begotten Son, that whoever believes in Him should not perish but have everlasting life. (John 3:16, NKJV)

This is my commandment, that you love one another as I have loved you. Greater love has no one than this, that someone lay down his life for his friends. You are my friends if you do what I command you. (John 15:12–14, ESV)

DAY 241

It's Time to Dream Again

If we are not careful, we find ourselves thinking about the past: what could or should have been, our dreams, plans, and desires that the Lord placed in our heart at the start of our journey with Him. A significant number of those dreams have been forgotten or have even died, leaving us disappointed and discouraged, and allowing depression to get a foothold in our lives. We can't live in the land of regret in a state of "What if?" We must believe that God has great things ahead and is able to resurrect His dreams for us.

It's resurrection time, and we all have different things in our lives that need to be resurrected. The word resurrection means being raised from the dead or coming back to life. In the Oxford Dictionary, to resurrect something is to "revive or revitalize (something that is inactive, disused, or forgotten)."[7] Some synonyms for "resurrect" listed at synonym.com include revive, restore or rejuvenate.[8]

There is a desert plant called the resurrection plant. When the plant is dry it forms into a tight ball, but when moistened it unfolds and blooms. It's resurrection time, so jump into the river of life and let God revive, restore, and renew all those dreams, desires, and plans you thought were dead, forgotten, and gone from your life. Some of us may be able to relate to the resurrection plant—finding ourselves in a dry place, curled up in a tight ball, and lying dormant—however, when moistened by His Spirit, those things that we thought were dead are going to unfold and bloom again. It's resurrection time, and ultimately this will lead to a harvest of souls!

> It seemed like a dream, too good to be true, when God returned Zion's exiles. We laughed, we sang, we couldn't believe our good fortune. We were the talk of the nations—"God was wonderful to them!" God was wonderful to us; we are one happy people.

And now, God, do it again—bring rain to our drought-stricken lives so those who planted their crops in despair will shout hurrahs at the harvest, So those who went off with heavy hearts will come home laughing, with armloads of blessings. (Psalm 126:1–6, MSG)

DAY 242

They Will Come to Their Senses

God is greater than anything! It's harvest time, and He is moving in amazing ways throughout the earth in response to the hunger in people's hearts. Don't ever stop telling others about the Lord, even if it doesn't seem like they care or are paying any attention to what you're saying. They will come to their senses as the Lord draws them by His Spirit. People throughout the earth are turning their lives over to God in greater numbers than ever before, so keep praising and thanking Him for the harvest.

Here's the story I will tell my friends when they come to worship, and punctuate it with Hallelujahs: Shout Hallelujah, you God-worshipers; give glory, you sons of Jacob; adore him, you daughters of Israel. He has never let you down, never looked the other way when you were being kicked around. He has never wandered off to do his own thing; he has been right there, listening.

Here in this great gathering for worship I have discovered this praise-life. And I'll do what I promised right here in front of the God-worshipers. Down-and-outers sit at God's table and eat their fill. Everyone on the hunt for God is here, praising him. "Live it up, from head to toe. Don't ever quit!"

From the four corners of the earth people are coming to their senses, are running back to God. Long lost-families are falling on their faces before him. God has taken charge; from now on he has the last word.

All the power-mongers are before him—worshiping! All the poor and powerless too—worshiping! Along with all those who never got it together—worshiping!

Our children and their children will get in on this as the word is passed along from parent to child. Babies not yet conceived will hear the good news—that God does what he says. (Psalm 22:22–31, MSG)

DAY 243

The Greatest of These Is Love

It is love that causes us to fall to our knees—love for the Father, Son, and Holy Spirit, love for our brothers and sisters in Christ, and love for lost humanity. It was love that caused Jesus to fall to His knees in the garden and cry out *"not my will but yours be done"* (Luke 22:42, NET). Love never ends, and it will never fail.

> *Three things will last forever—faith, hope, and love—and the greatest of these is love.* (1 Corinthians 13:13, NLT)

We need to be knee soldiers, because the harvest will not be realized without a fight! The battle will be won with prayers filled with faith, hope, and love.

DAY 244

Time to Dream Again

Two things are continually happening on earth—people are being born and people are dying.

Everything that happens in this world happens at the time God chooses.

He sets time for birth and the time for death, the time for planting and the time for pulling up, the time for killing and the time for healing, the time for tearing down and the time for building. He sets the time for sorrow and the time for joy, the time for mourning and for dancing. (Ecclesiastes 3:1–4, GNT)

Although birth and death are natural events, they are primarily spiritual in nature. I have recently experienced a season of death for some of my dreams, but also the resurrection, birthing, and conception of new ones.

Dreams, visions, and desires are conceived in our hearts, and just like with a natural pregnancy, things don't always go as planned. Sometimes in pregnancy a miscarriage happens. A miscarriage isn't planned—it is an unexpected death that is sometimes called a spontaneous abortion. One meaning of "miscarriage" listed on dictionary.com is "failure to attain the just, right, or desired result."[9] Our dreams, visions, and plans can be spontaneously aborted when desired results are not obtained and we never reach the place of birthing them. This is not our fault or choice, but there are other times when we purposely abort them. In those situations, it's our choice to let the dreams die or to not come to fruition. The birthing process isn't easy, and that's why we need a coach—someone to come alongside and encourage us to help bring those things into being.

When a miscarriage takes place, a dream is gone, but it doesn't mean you cannot conceive again. Some dreams can be reborn, resurrected, and brought back to life, while others cannot. It might feel like we are forever pregnant or in labour for a long time, but just keep believing—God wants you to birth those things that He caused to be conceived. You will eventually come to full term and give birth, because a pregnancy doesn't last forever. God has given the Holy Spirit and other believers to help us, so don't quit or give up! Labour isn't easy, but the results are awesome.

When the Lord brought back the captivity of Zion, We were like those who dream. Then our mouth was filled with laughter, And our tongue with singing. Then they said among the nations, "The Lord has done great things for them." The Lord has done great things for us, And we are glad. (Psalm 126:1–3, NKJV)

DAY 245

It Is Never Too Late

One night I had a dream that I was in a doctor's office and was told that I was pregnant. I said to the doctor, "That's impossible—I'm too old to have a baby!"

His reply was "Well, you are pregnant." He proceeded to inform me that at my age it was unsafe for me to remain pregnant and there was a high likelihood that the baby would not be normal, so I should have an abortion.

A friend with me blurted out, "No way—she isn't too old! The baby will be born healthy! We'll take care of her and make sure she takes it easy and gets enough rest."

Don't let the enemy tell you to abort your dreams. Some dreams die through miscarriage, which is no fault of your own. The enemy will lie and tell you it is too late or you are too old, but don't listen to him—he is a liar. It's never too late with God!

> *Now indeed, Elizabeth your relative has also conceived a son in her old age; and this is now the sixth month for her who was called barren. For with God nothing will be impossible.* (Luke 1:36–37, NKJV)

DAY 246

Stay the Course

In life, things can happen without warning that force us to go in a whole different direction. We find our faith and trust in God and everything we believe challenged in ways it never was before. We need to make a choice to keep going, stay the course, and continue trusting in God. When we find ourselves in difficult circumstances, there is an unbelievable array of emotions that will try and overwhelm us.

I found myself in one of those unexpected, hard situations when I was in Kenya on a missions trip. It was my birthday, and I had just gone to bed after spending the day ministering to many children. I had been given one of the best presents ever as those precious children sang happy birthday to me in both English and their language, and we had a fun-filled day of games, music, crafts, teaching them about the baptism in the Holy Spirit, and praying and ministering to them. We were on a spiritual high when I got a phone call that my husband had taken his life, and it changed my whole life in an instant. In some ways, it was easier to deal with then than it was several months later, as God's grace just took over in the moment.

God's love and grace are amazing beyond words. I am always astounded how He carries us through times like that. I have asked God many times since that day, "Why?" It's something I will never totally understand this side of heaven. Some days "why" doesn't seem to matter, while other times it does. There is much we can learn through life's trials if we allow God to teach us, and we can take what we have been taught and help others.

If you are struggling, talk to someone, don't put up walls, and don't isolate yourself—that's what the enemy wants, because we are stronger when we stand together. We were never meant to deal with the struggles of this life alone. No matter where you find yourself today, no matter what life throws your way, God is greater. We can overcome anything—and I do mean anything.

For every child of God defeats this evil world, and we achieve this victory through our faith. And who can win this battle against the world? Only those who believe that Jesus is the Son of God. (1 John 5:4–5, NLT)

DAY 247

Dining with the King

There is nothing better than dining with the King of Kings—it's a smorgasbord of all you can eat and drink, and it's free. It's top of the line nutrition for your spirit that will give you the lift and strength you need to stand strong against any trial that comes your way.

> *Listen! Whoever is thirsty, come to the water! Whoever has no money can come, buy, and eat! Come, buy wine and milk. You don't have to pay; it's free! Why do you spend money on what cannot nourish you and your wages on what does not satisfy you? Listen carefully to me: Eat what is good, and enjoy the best foods. Open your ears and come to me! Listen so that you may live!...*
>
> *Seek the Lord while he may be found. Call on him while he is near.* (Isaiah 55:1–3a, 6, GW)

"I am the bread of life," Jesus told them. "Those who come to me will never be hungry; those who believe in me will never be thirsty." (John 6:35, GNT)

DAY 248

We Must Die So He Can Live

Precious in the sight of the Lord is the death of His saints. (Psalm 116:15, NKJV)

It is hard to see death as something precious, because death is an enemy. It seems even more so when the person hasn't had a chance to live a full life on this earth. However, we don't really die. Our physical body does, but our spirit lives forever. What makes the death of a saint so precious to the Lord is when we die to self—when our old sin nature dies and we take on His nature and drink daily of the cup of salvation. We must die so He can live!

What shall I render to the Lord for all his benefits towards me? I will take up the cup of salvation, And call upon the name of the Lord. (Psalm 116:12–13, NKJV)

Jesus said to all of them, "If people want to follow me, they must give up the things they want. They must be willing to give up their lives daily to follow me." (Luke 9:23, NCV)

DAY 249

The Loudest Voice in Any Storm

God's voice may be small and quiet sometimes, but it should be the loudest and clearest voice we hear in any storm or battle. When we acknowledge and worship Him in the storm, His voice will be heard loud and clear above the thunder of the waves.

> *Acknowledge the majesty of the Lord's reputation! Worship the Lord in holy attire! The Lord's voice is heard over the water; the majestic God thunders, the Lord appears over the surging water. The Lord's shout is powerful. The Lord's shout is majestic. The Lord's shout breaks the cedars, the Lord shatters the cedars of Lebanon.... The Lord's shout strikes with flaming fire. The Lord's shout shakes the wilderness, the Lord shakes the wilderness of Kadesh. The Lord's shout bends the large trees and strips the leaves from the forests. Everyone in his temple says, "Majestic!" The Lord sits enthroned over the engulfing waters, the Lord sits enthroned as the eternal king.* (Psalm 29:2–4, 7–10, NET)

DAY 250

Turn It All Over to God

We hear people say things like this all the time: "I am so stressed, so overwhelmed, so burned out." It may be true, but most of the time it's our own fault, because we take on more than we are able to handle. Sometimes the problem isn't even that we're taking on too much, but that we're trying to do everything in our own ability; this causes us to worry and become anxious or fearful, which leads to oppression, depression, and hopelessness.

We have to say "no" sometimes, and learn how to cast our cares upon the Lord as the Bible tells us. In this life, we all face difficulties, challenges, trials, and storms. But the Lord is always there, ready to help when troubles come our way, and His grace is sufficient for us. We just need to take the time to sit at His feet, pray, and listen to Him.

In the Gospel of Luke 10:41–42, when Martha complained about her sister not helping her do the work, Jesus told her that she was *"troubled about many things"* (NET) but that Mary had chosen wisely. Mary chose to spend time with Jesus and not to concern herself with doing for the Lord—it was enough to just be with Him.

The greatest antidote to stress is casting everything on the Lord and spending time with Him. Everything gets done more quickly and easily in an atmosphere of peace, and we hear His voice more clearly. I haven't always cast all my cares on the Lord, but I'm learning more and more to do this and it makes the journey easier and more enjoyable. While we live on this earth, we'll continually have to deal with difficult situations, so we might as well respond with joy. When trials come, we can choose to allow the Lord's grace, mercy, peace, love, and joy to overtake us and carry us through the storms. God wants us to enjoy the journey!

Turn all your anxiety over to God because he cares for you. Keep your mind clear, and be alert. Your opponent the devil is prowling around like a roaring lion as he looks for someone to devour. Be firm in the faith and resist him, knowing that other believers throughout the world are going through the same kind of suffering. God, who shows you his kindness and who has called you through Christ Jesus to his eternal glory, will restore you, strengthen you, make you strong, and support you as you suffer for a little while. (1 Peter 5:7–10, GW)

Then Jesus said, "Come to me, all you who are weary and carry heavy burdens, and I will give you rest. Take my yoke upon you. Let me teach you, because I am humble and gentle at heart, and you will find rest for your souls. For my yoke is easy to bear, and the burden I give you is light." (Matthew 11:28–30, NLT)

DAY 251

What's Damming Up the River?

I was singing about the floodgates of heaven opening and allowing the rain of the Spirit to come, and I heard in my spirit, "The dam's about to burst." We all have dams inside of us that are stopping or hindering the flow of the Spirit in our lives. A dam is a barrier constructed to hold back the water and raise its level. It's a confined body of water that obstructs or hinders the flow of the water. It's time to open the floodgates of our hearts and let the river flow out of us.

A good question to ask is "What's damming up the river of His Spirit from flowing in our lives?" There are many things that could obstruct the flow. Some obvious hindrances are fear, unforgiveness, jealousy, complacency, and feelings of unworthiness. We need to repent and stop allowing those barriers to hold back the waters of His Spirit from rising within us. We need to choose to open the floodgates and let the dam burst in our lives. It's our choice to stop damming the river. When we allow the floodgates to open, the river will bring refreshing to us and salvation to others.

> *Wherever the river flows, every living thing that moves will thrive. There will be great schools of fish, because when these waters enter the sea, it will be fresh. Wherever the river flows, everything will live.* (Ezekiel 47:9, CEB)

> *He who believes in Me [who cleaves to and trusts in and relies on Me] as the Scripture has said, From his innermost being shall flow [continuously] springs and rivers of living water.* (John 7:38, AMPC)

DAY 252

Get Rid of the Garbage

It's time to get rid of the garbage in our lives. Garbage smells bad when left around, and it can stink up the whole house. When we lived on our acreage we had an ongoing issue with garbage; we had to burn it, take it to the dump, or put it in our neighbours' Loraas bin. We only had to walk across the road to dispose of it in the container, but often it seemed to take a while to make it there.

It's time to rid our lives of stinkin' thinkin'. We allow wrong thoughts to invade our minds, so we need to cast them down and rid our lives of them. We let them ferment and rot until they permeate our whole being—so dump them out right away. It's easier to get rid of one bag of garbage at a time than waiting until it piles up! There are always going to be wrong thoughts that we have to rid our minds of—we can't ignore them or they will pile up, creating a huge mess in our lives.

> *For though we live in the body, we do not wage war in an unspiritual way, since the weapons of our warfare are not worldly, but are powerful through God for the demolition of strongholds. We demolish arguments and every high-minded thing that is raised up against the knowledge of God, taking every thought captive to obey Christ. (2 Corinthians 10:3–5, HCSB)*

> *Don't fret or worry. Instead of worrying, pray. Let petitions and praises shape your worries into prayers, letting God know your concerns. Before you know it, a sense of God's wholeness, everything coming together for good, will come and settle you down. It's wonderful what happens when Christ displaces worry at the center of your life.*

Summing it all up, friends, I'd say you'll do best by filling your minds and meditating on things true, noble, reputable, authentic, compelling, gracious—the best, not the worst; the beautiful, not the ugly; things to praise, not things to curse. (Philippians 4:6–8, MSG)

DAY 253

Let the Wind of the Spirit Blow

One day I went for a walk with a friend to the weir and across the train bridge. We were laughing at how windy it was and sliding down the stairs on the bike lift. As we walked, laughing and enjoying ourselves, I couldn't help but think about how refreshing the wind was as we breathed in the cool fresh air.

The wind of His Spirit is so refreshing—there's nothing like it. It's like a breath of fresh air, renewing and reviving, and it's fun to just let the wind blow on you. God's breath brings dreams and desires back to life, and brings the life of God to spiritually dead people.

> *He then told me to say: Dry bones, listen to what the Lord is saying to you, "I, the Lord God, will put breath in you, and once again you will live. I will wrap you with muscles and skin and breathe life into you. Then you will know that I am the Lord."*
>
> *I did what the Lord said, but before I finished speaking, I heard a rattling noise. The bones were coming together! I saw muscles and skin cover the bones, but they had no life in them.*
>
> *The Lord said: Ezekiel, now say to the wind, "The Lord God commands you to blow from every direction and to breathe life into these dead bodies, so they can live again."*
>
> *As soon as I said this, the wind blew among the bodies, and they came back to life! They all stood up, and there were enough to make a large army.* (Ezekiel 37:4–10, CEV)

The wind of God is blowing, and a vast army is arising as we allow His Spirit to blow in and through our lives!

DAY 254

A Picture of Unity

God uses nature to teach us about spiritual things. A friend and I were walking by the river the other day, watching the geese and talking about how they flew as one and were a great picture of unity. There were many geese on an island in the river and it looked very full, but then another flock came and flew above the island a couple of times. It became very noisy as both the geese on the ground and those in the sky began honking. We thought the second flock was going to fly away as there was no room for them to land, but then they started to fly downward and the geese on the ground made room for them. As we walked along we looked back and saw this happen a few more times. It amazed us how many geese could fit on one small island. We watched as different flocks came together, making room for each other as they gathered for one purpose: to fly south. They instinctively understand that there is safety in numbers. The larger the group, the easier it is to fly long distances without tiring, because the wind current produced becomes stronger, carrying them along.

As churches come together, making room for our differences and helping one another to achieve our goals, the wind of His Spirit will become stronger. This will cause a synergy amongst us so we won't tire or burn out. Like the geese, there is really one goal, and that is to see all humanity come to a saving knowledge of Jesus Christ so the Glory of God will cover the earth.

> *Always be humble and gentle. Patiently put up with each other and love each other. Try your best to let God's Spirit keep your hearts united. Do this by living at peace. All of you are part of the same body. There is only one Spirit of God, just as you were given*

one hope when you were chosen to be God's people. We have only one Lord, one faith, and one baptism. There is one God who is the Father of all people. Not only is God above all others, but he works by using all of us, and he lives in all of us. (Ephesians 4:2–6, CEV)

DAY 255

Let the Walls Fall Down

We all have walls in our lives that need to come down. God wants us to go into our promised land, but first the walls of addiction, fear, sickness, oppression, etc., have to fall. In order for the walls to fall we need to see as God sees, allowing Him to take us to another level of revelation.

Joshua saw differently. In the book of Joshua it tells us that he looked and he saw. Joshua needed to have a transformation in his seeing to be able to move to the next level and take Jericho. Joshua was told that the man who appeared to him was the commander of the Lord's army; he received insight about the man, and he listened to him and obeyed his orders. We have to look, see, and believe that Jesus came to set us free from anything that hinders us. Otherwise, we won't have the faith for walls to crumble in our lives—something that will truly take our faith to another level.

> *When Joshua was by Jericho, he lifted up his eyes and looked, and behold, a man was standing before him with his drawn sword in his hand. And Joshua went to him and said to him, "Are you for us, or for our adversaries?" And he said, "No; but I am the commander of the army of the Lord. Now I have come." And Joshua fell on his face to the earth and worshiped and said to him, "What does my lord say to his servant?"* (Joshua 5:13–14, ESV)

It's time for the walls to fall, and for us to take hold of and possess all that God has promised us!

DAY 256

Stagnant Faith

One day I was just sitting in my office at work and I heard these two words: "stagnant faith." The problem with some people is that their faith has become stagnant. When something is stagnant, it isn't flowing or moving—it's inactive.

Faith has to be acted upon. Immobile faith doesn't produce any results. We all have faith—no matter how small—but some believers have let theirs become inactive, not developing or advancing in it. If we don't continually use our faith, it can become unproductive. In Hebrews 11 (NKJV), over and over it says, *"By faith Noah…"* (verse 7), *"By faith Abraham…"* (verse 17), *"By faith the walls of Jericho fell down…"* (verse 30). It was by faith that Peter walked on the water.

But be doers of the word, and not hearers only, deceiving yourselves. (James 1:22, NKJV)

If we don't want our faith to go stagnant, we need to act on the Word of God and obey the leading of the Holy Spirit.

DAY 257

Eyes Fixed on Jesus

Above all else, the Lord wants to be the centre of our lives. But the only way He can be is if we keep our eyes fixed on Him! The words in this song by Helen Howard Lemmel perfectly describe this:

> Turn your eyes upon Jesus,
> Look full in His wonderful face,
> And the things of earth will grow strangely dim,
> In the light of His glory and grace.

You will keep him in perfect peace, Whose mind is stayed on you... (Isaiah 26:3, NKJV)

Be thankful the Lord is our peace, right in the middle of the storm we face. It may be chaotic all around you, but inside, you can have complete peace. Keep your eyes fixed on the Lord! Jesus said that Martha was troubled about many things. Why? Her eyes weren't fixed on Jesus.

Then He arose and rebuked the wind, and said to the sea, "Peace, be still!" And the wind ceased and there was a great calm.... "Who can this be, that even the wind and the sea obey Him!" (Mark 4:39, 41b, NKJV)

Jesus is our Prince of Peace, the centre of our lives, and the place we fix our eyes!

DAY 258

We Never Can Be Too Thankful

We have so much to be thankful for. Many times, I have woken up thinking about how good God is—there's no better way to start the day. God's goodness surrounds us continually, and His mercy will last forever.

> …thank God no matter what happens. This is the way God wants you who belong to Christ Jesus to live. (1 Thessalonians 5:18, MSG)

A thankful heart is a blessed heart; we have so much to be thankful for, no matter what. David was a man after God's own heart—he was a man of prayer, and a worshipper who lived a lifestyle of thankfulness.

> Thank you! Everything in me says "Thank you!" Angels listen as I sing my thanks. I kneel in worship facing your holy temple and say it again: "Thank you!" Thank you for your love, thank you for your faithfulness; Most holy is your name, most holy is your Word. The moment I called out, you stepped in; you made my life large with strength.
>
> When they hear what you have to say, God, all earth's kings will say "Thank you." They'll sing of what you've done: "How great the glory of God!" And here's why: God, high above, sees far below; no matter the distance, he knows everything about us.
>
> When I walk into the thick of trouble, keep me alive in the angry turmoil. With one hand strike my foes, With your other hand save me. Finish what you started in me, God. Your love is eternal—don't quit on me now. (Psalm 138, MSG)

Be thankful, because God never gives up on us! We can never be too thankful!

DAY 259

We Have Authority

One day I found myself thinking about bugs—someone had said to me that they were fighting a bug, or in medical terms, a virus. Bugs are annoying, pesky things. For many years we lived across the road from a dairy barn, and every fall there was an invasion of flies. I would keep all the doors and windows closed, but somehow they always managed to get in. The "swatting anointing" would come upon me, and I could get several at one time.

We need to learn to swat those nasty flu and cold bugs with the sword of the Spirit—the Word of God. When my kids were young and caught one of those viruses, we would sing this little song I'd made up with them.

Speak, speak, speak the Word,
Speak the Word each day;
Speak, speak, speak the Word,
Sickness runs away!

A good example is what happened with the Ebola virus—many people were full of fear, but instead of being afraid, we believers need to take authority over it. When there is an outbreak of illness like that, there is a lot of fear that comes with it, but the world needs to see believers operating in the authority they have been given in these situations.

Behold, I give you the authority to trample on serpents and scorpions, and over all the power of the enemy, and nothing shall by any means hurt you. (Luke 10:19, NKJV)

DAY 260
Choose to Think God's Way

God is love, and He is good! There is nothing negative or toxic about Him; He radiates goodness. Thinking and responding negatively to any situation in life is our choice. We have the nature of our heavenly Father, whose character is always positive and good.

Then God said, "Let Us make man in Our image..." (Genesis 1:26a, NKJV)

This verse refers to the Father, Son, and Holy Spirit.

There is no fear in love; but perfect love casts out fear... (1 John 4:18a, NKJV)

It's obvious that we choose to fear and to experience negative emotions. That's why people react in such different ways when the storms of life come. We are amazed because one person gets down, depressed, or overwhelmed, while another seems to handle their situation in a positive way with joy, peace, and love. Well, these differences are because one chooses to react negatively and the other chooses to respond God's way.

We need to see like God and learn to respond in the way He created us to. We don't have to allow the negative, toxic thoughts of this world to control our response.

Children, you belong to God, and you have defeated these enemies. God's Spirit is in you and is more powerful than the one that is in the world. (1 John 4:4, CEV)

I've told you this so that my peace will be with you. In the world you'll have trouble. But cheer up! I have overcome the world. (John 16:33, GW)

DAY 261

Peace in the Midst of the Storm

One weekend I was on my way to a women's conference when I had an interesting experience. It was the first snowfall of the winter. I had driven into the city from my acreage and was pleased because the road conditions were good, but the streets in the city itself were very icy.

I had picked up a couple of friends and was en route to get one more when the person sitting in the front passenger seat said, "What is that truck doing?" There was a truck turning at an intersection in front of us, and even under good conditions it shouldn't have turned. We were too close.

I calmly said, "I don't know what he is doing." I never braked, but kept driving the same slow speed and went right by him. I looked to the side as I passed and the vehicle couldn't have been more than an inch away from my car.

The other ladies were saying "In Jesus' Name," and I kept driving like I was oblivious to the danger. There was no fear or panic—it was complete peace and calm, as the Lord was in control!

If we react that way every time a storm or circumstance comes our way, we will just sail through unscathed. I believe those of us in the car reacted that way because each of us has a strong relationship with the Lord and was confident that God was with us in the car: as our peace, our protector, and strong tower. Fear and panic couldn't even enter the picture.

You will keep him in perfect peace, Whose mind is stayed on You, Because he trusts in you. (Isaiah 26:3, NKJV)

DAY 262

Praise Him

I so love it when I wake up with these words on my mind, "There is no one like my God, and I will praise Him." There couldn't be any truer words—no one compares to Him! He is our All in All, and more than enough. He is our Creator, Protector, Healer, the Great I Am, the King of Kings, the Alpha and the Omega, the Beginning and the End. He is our Prince of Peace; he is Wisdom, the Joy-Giver, Living Water, our Salvation, and our soon and coming King! And that doesn't even begin to describe Him!

He is more than we can imagine, and we are everything to Him! Oh, how he loves us so! He is worthy of glory and honour and praise!

I will bless the Lord at all times; His praise shall continually be in my mouth. (Psalm 34:1, NKJV)

Bless the Lord, O my soul; And all that is within me, bless His Holy Name! (Psalm 103:1, NKJV)

Praise the Lord, all you servants of the Lord, all who stand in the house of the Lord night after night. Lift your hands toward the holy place, and praise the Lord. (Psalm 134:1–2, GW)

DAY 263

When Will You Make the Choice?

We always hear people say, "I am too busy," but being busy isn't really the problem. It's that we don't do busy well. The only way we can successfully manage everything we do is to make the Lord the centre of everything. We need to be in continual communication with the Lord.

Another word for communication with the Lord is prayer! Prayer is a lifestyle—we should live a life of prayer. Prayer isn't just something we do when we find ourselves in a tough spot or in an unexpected storm. Storms are going to come no matter what. Prayer might get us through the storm, but prayer and praise are things we should do before the storm, during the storm, and after the storm. Prayer, worship, and joyful praise should be our first response in any situation. This will keep those toxic thoughts away.

> *Always be joyful. Never stop praying. Be thankful in all circumstances, for this is God's will for you who belong to Christ Jesus.* (1 Thessalonians 5:16–18, NLT)

I can only use my own life as an example, but when Clarence went to heaven my initial response really set the course of my thinking—even to this day. People think we aren't normal if we don't grieve. How can we be content and joyful under very difficult circumstances? By the way we choose to think about a situation, and whether we allow God into the storm with us. We can find good in any situation. I made a choice to pray, praise, worship, and rejoice. You would be amazed at what we can find to rejoice about in the middle of a storm. The more we rejoice, the more we find to rejoice about. One of my first thoughts was that my husband was in heaven, and since Jesus had carried my sorrow I didn't have to carry it myself.

The Bible helps us change toxic, negative thoughts into positive, uplifting ones. Does that mean difficult moments don't happen? No—I have difficult times, but when I encourage myself in the Lord my thinking changes. If I had chosen to become angry, upset, unforgiving, fearful, or grief-stricken when my husband died, I would be in a completely different place today. This doesn't mean that I didn't have to deal with feelings of anger, unforgiveness, and grief—I still do—but I just made a choice not to live there. I am no different than anyone else; we can all make the choice to think correctly, but we can't do it without God.

Why am I discouraged? Why is my heart so sad? I will put my hope in God! I will praise him again—my Savior and my God! (Psalm 43:5, NLT)

DAY 264

Be Continually Connected

My favourite topic is prayer. I love prayer for a lot of different reasons. There is nothing like praising or singing—nothing like worshipping God.

I know that one of the toughest things to deal with when you lose a loved one, especially a spouse, is loneliness. All we need to do, though, is realize we are never alone. Start praising God, and His presence will overwhelm you, causing loneliness to dissipate. There is nothing like the presence of the King. Prayer and praise are the connection, the telephone line to heaven. It's our choice if we want to be continually connected or not.

People wonder how they can pray continually when life is so busy, but that question indicates wrong thinking about what prayer is. There are several different ways to pray. There are times that I call concentrated prayer when you set a time aside, corporately or personally, to intercede for specific people or situations, or to read the Word of God, or just sit quietly and let God speak.

We also need to have an attitude or spirit of prayer, being continually aware of God. We know that He is available, and we can call upon Him continually throughout our day. We get too busy for Him, but He is never too busy for us. It's just like when you're expecting an important phone call—you are ready and waiting for that call. I believe the Lord is ready and waiting for us to call, day or night!

> *I will praise you, my God and King, and always honor your name. I will praise you each day and always honor your name. You are wonderful, Lord, and you deserve all praise, because you are much greater than anyone can understand.* (Psalm 145:1–3, CEV)

The Lord is near to all who call upon Him, To all who call upon Him in truth.... My mouth shall speak the praise of the Lord, And all flesh shall bless His holy name forever and ever. (Psalm 145:18, 21, NKJV)

DAY 265

The Holy Spirit Is a Singing Spirit

There are many different attributes of the Holy Spirit. One characteristic is that the Holy Spirit is a singing Spirit. He puts a song in our heart, a song of praise to our God. He gives us songs to sing to encourage us, to build us up. When you find yourself in a difficult situation, like Paul and Silas did, just start singing. It is what I did when I found myself in very difficult circumstances. When you do this, you will find your life overcome by His love, joy, peace, grace, and mercy. The Holy Spirit truly becomes your comfort!

> *...speaking to one another in psalms and hymns and spiritual songs, singing and making melody in your heart to the Lord...*
> (Ephesians 5:19, NKJV)

DAY 266
Healthy Thoughts, Healthy Results

How we think really does affect our lives! Recently, a friend showed me a video of an amazing gymnast who, incredibly, had been born without legs. Her adopted parents acted on a Biblical truth when they modelled the attitude of "never say can't" for her.

How we think determines how we speak and what we say, and what we say determines our actions. Toxic thoughts produce negative outcomes, whereas healthy thoughts produce positive outcomes. By not allowing the gymnast to say "can't," her parents formed an attitude in her that she could overcome anything.

Negative thinking is formed when we entertain thoughts of being taken advantage of. Thirty years ago, we met a quiet introvert and got along well with him. As the years passed, he began to believe we had somehow wronged him. His thoughts progressed from jealousy to anger and hatred to murder. Many years later he eventually acted on a plan to harm our family, but God intervened and kept us safe.

Negative thinking causes our mind to become toxic—our brain becomes ill. Mental illness is just as much an illness as a physical illness. As believers, we need to think, speak, and act according to the Word of God.

Finally, brethren, whatever things are true, whatever things are noble, whatever things are just, whatever things are pure, whatever things are lovely, whatever things are of good report, if there is any virtue and if there is anything praiseworthy—meditate on these things. (Philippians 4:8, NKJV)

God's way in the only way to live a healthy, productive, and fulfilled life!

DAY 267
Our Guiding Light

Who dominates your life? I have found that what really makes the difference is letting the Spirit dominate from within. Let the Spirit of God lead you, and you'll never go wrong. The Holy Spirit is our helper. If we learn to obey His promptings, we will be able to overcome anything. Whether health issues, a financial need, addictions, fear, anger, rejection, or a bad habit, we can change anything with the Spirit's help.

The more time we spend in His presence, the more we will obey His voice and His inner promptings. Let His Spirit rise within you until it dominates everything else.

> *The spirit of man is the lamp of the Lord, searching all his innermost parts.* (Proverbs 20:27, ESV)

> *For You will light my lamp; the Lord my God will enlighten my darkness.* (Psalm 18:28, NKJV)

The Spirit of God is our helper and our guide. Let His Spirit be your guiding light!

DAY 268

Change is Inevitable

People always talk about change. They either like it or hate it, but in life, change is inevitable! I used to think that I handled change well, but now I realize that I only liked the change that I could control or choose myself. We don't like it when change happens unexpectedly, causing situations we haven't chosen for ourselves. When we are aware that circumstances are changing, though, we can prepare ourselves to go with the change.

It's much easier to walk in the light than the dark. Holding onto our past is like trying to walk in the dark. Whether change comes from us voluntarily grabbing hold of it or because it is necessary, we need to make sure to yield to the will of God. His grace helps us move forward, and His Spirit shows us how to make the necessary changes in our lives.

Make your ways known to me, Lord; teach me your paths. Lead me in your truth—teach it to me—because you are the God who saves me. I put my hope in you all day long. (Psalm 25:4–5, CEB)

DAY 269

We Need Each Other

Today I helped boost someone's car. In life, we need others to give us a boost from time to time. We need believers to encourage us to get into God's presence so we can have our battery charged up once again. Just like it's impossible to boost our own car, we need other believers to help us recognize that we need to get to God, our power source.

> *If you fall, your friend can help you up. But if you fall without having a friend nearby, you are really in trouble.* (Ecclesiastes 4:10, CEV)

DAY 270
Choose to Enter In

Today was one of those days I woke up with such an overwhelming joy in my heart. God is so good!

Shout happily to the Lord, all the earth. Serve the Lord cheerfully. Come into his presence with a joyful song. Realize that the Lord alone is God. He made us, and we are his. We are his people and the sheep in his care. Enter his gates with a song of thanksgiving. Come into his courtyards with a song of praise. Give thanks to him; praise his name.
The Lord is good. His mercy endures forever. His faithfulness endures throughout every generation. (Psalm 100, GW)

I noticed while reading these verses that "gates" and "courtyards" are in the plural form. God has a special place in His presence for each one of us. We can all go in together, but we individually have to choose to enter his gates with thanksgiving and his courts with praise. We each have a personal relationship with God—so there is a gate for you to enter and a courtyard for you to come into. We encourage each other to enter into God's presence, but our choice is an individual one. We can't prevent others from entering in if we don't choose to, but when we enter together His manifested presence is even more powerful.

Together we produce synergy when we enter into God's presence. Synergy is defined by the Business Dictionary as "a state in which two or more things work together in a particularly fruitful way that produces an effect greater than the sum of their individual effects."[10] Cooperation through the choice to work together will lead to a powerful and effective time in God's presence.

We choose to rejoice today because the Lord has made it just for us! There is nothing like the presence of the King!

DAY 271

He Is Never Too Busy —Just Call

One thing that I appreciate about living alone is that I get to spend lots of time with the Lord. One of my favourite things to do is to sing and worship the Lord. His presence has been my saving grace since my husband passed away. There is no one like my God—He really is my all in all!

If you are feeling brokenhearted, lonely, or depressed, just call out to the Lord. He is always available and will answer you. We never get a busy signal or a voice saying, "Unable to take your call," or "Please stay on the line and I will answer as soon I am available." God is never too busy, and He won't ever put you on hold. He wants to talk with you all the time.

We can make prayer seem like a difficult thing. Some people stress over not spending a whole hour in the morning with the Lord, but prayer isn't developed through rigid practices. We should spend time with the Lord every day in prayer, worship, and His Word. These things should be a part of our daily lifestyle—not something we have to do, but something we get to do! We always want there to be an open line of communication between heaven and earth: times of deep conversation and casual discussion, as there are in any relationship. We don't want to get so caught up in doing for the Lord that we forget the most significant part—being with Him!

"When you call out to me and come to me in prayer, I will hear your prayers. When you seek me in prayer and worship, you will

find me available to you. If you seek me with all your heart and soul, I will make myself available to you," says the Lord. (Jeremiah 29:12–14a, NET)

DAY 272

Thanksgiving—the Key to His Presence

I recently had a song on my heart written by Don Moen, "I Just Want to Be Where You Are." I haven't sung it for years, but it should be the cry of our hearts. The song talks about our desire to draw near to the Lord and dwell in His presence daily.

God's presence is our dwelling place. He wants us to live there—to make His presence our home. It's not a vacation home or a cabin on the lake where we go to relax a few times a year. His presence is our permanent residence, the place where we live daily. All we need to do is unlock the front door, as we do every day to enter our home. Thanksgiving is the key to entering God's presence.

Surely the righteous shall give thanks to Your name; The upright shall dwell in Your presence. (Psalm 140:13, NKJV)

DAY 273

Engrave the Word on the Tablet of Your Heart

The Word of God needs to be engraved on our very hearts, and not just written there. Writing can be covered, erased, or changed, whereas an engraving is permanent. The Word of God has great significance in our lives.

> *Indeed, your written instructions make me happy. They are my best friends....*
> *O Lord, your word is established in heaven forever....*
> *Oh, how I love your teachings! They are in my thoughts all day long. Your commandments make me wiser than my enemies, because your commandments are always with me....*
> *You are my hiding place and my shield. My hope is based on your word....*
> *Your word is a doorway that lets in light, and it helps gullible people understand....*
> *Trouble and hardship have found me, but your commandments still make me happy....*
> *There is lasting peace for those who love your teachings. Nothing can make those people stumble.* (Psalm 119:24, 89, 97–98, 114, 130, 143, 165, GW)

God's Word gives us wisdom, direction, protection, joy, peace, and so much more as we engrave it on the tablet of our heart.

DAY 274

Power in the Name

An old hymn, "All Hail the Power of Jesus' Name," written by Edward Perronet, came to mind as I was driving home today:

All hail the power of Jesus' Name!
Let angels prostrate fall,
Bring forth the royal diadem,
And crown Him Lord of all!

An acquaintance told me about a recent medical scare that had taken place in their body, and how they cried out in the Name of Jesus and the symptoms left them immediately. There is power in the Name of Jesus! He is Lord over all sickness, fear, and anything else that could come against us. This reminds me of the story of Peter and John and the man at Jerusalem's Beautiful Gate:

Then Peter said, "Silver and gold I do not have, but what I do have I give you: in the name of Jesus Christ of Nazareth, rise up and walk." (Acts 3:6, NKJV)

It was the power of his name that gave strength to this lame man. What you see and know was done by faith in his name; it was faith in Jesus that has made him well, as you can all see. (Acts 3:16, GNT)

We as believers should know that there is power in Jesus' Name. My acquaintance had questioned whether calling on His name really works, but God showed Himself mightily in that situation. God is so good, and He wants people to know that He is real—that He loves them and will answer when they call on His Name.

DAY 275

Always Available and Wanting to Help

God is beyond description—there is no one like Him. The God of the universe lives inside of us by His Spirit. His Spirit dwells inside our spirit. He is constantly available to us. He truly is our helper, counsellor, guide, teacher, revealer of truth, comforter, and so much more. The Holy Spirit came on the Old Testament prophets, but He lives in us! There is nothing we can't do with God's Spirit residing within us. He is the helper within, always available and eager to help.

> *The Spirit shows what is true and will come and guide you into the full truth. The Spirit doesn't speak on his own. He will tell you only what he has heard from me, and He will let you know what is going to happen.* (John 16:13, CEV)

DAY 276
Take His Prescription Daily

Do you ever get frustrated? Once, I was wide-awake in the middle of the night but really wanting to sleep, and I finally said out of frustration, "What do I need to do?"

I heard the Lord say, "Take your prescription," and He didn't mean medication or vitamins. I knew instantly what God was talking about. What I needed was a good dose of His presence.

Our daily prescription of the Word of God, prayer, praise, and worship brings us into His very presence. It's when we are in communication with Him that we see from God's perspective, which causes us to think, hear, and see correctly. We can never overdose on God's prescription—it's one addiction we want to hang onto, because it gives us strength! We have joy in God's presence and it becomes our strength.

> *But those who wait for the Lord [who expect, look for, and hope in Him] shall change and renew their strength and power; they shall lift their wings and mount up [close to God] as eagles [mount up to the sun]; they shall run and not be weary, they shall walk and not faint or become tired.* (Isaiah 40:31, AMPC)

DAY 277

The Fight of Faith

God created everything for a purpose, including the fish of the sea. Every October in the Adams River in British Columbia, hundreds of sockeye salmon return from the Pacific Ocean to spawn. I never thought as a child that it was anything special, but it really is.

People come from all over the world to see the salmon run. The sockeye salmon are born in the river and they swim all the way to the Pacific Ocean, where they live for the next four years and then instinctively return to the same place to lay their eggs and die. The young salmon have great determination, strength, endurance, and fight in them, as reaching the ocean isn't easy and many don't make it. Many of those that do reach the ocean are killed by predators or caught by fishermen.

The salmon that survive those four years begin to fight their way back upstream to where they were born. There are many obstacles in their path that make their journey very difficult, such as swimming against the current and rapids. British Columbia Fisheries built fish ladders in the Fraser River to help the salmon get through a place called Hells Gate, where there are rapids, strong currents, and very turbulent water. If they don't make it up the fish ladder on the first try, they will keep going back until they make it through.

God has given them this instinct to never give up. Their goal is to fulfill the purpose they were created for. It doesn't matter how many obstacles stand in their way, they never quit or give up. If a fish has enough fight, determination, and strength to not quit until they reach their goal, how much more should we! They would rather die trying than give up and go back to the ocean. Our fight is a fight of faith, so don't ever quit or turn back. Keep fighting, no matter the amount of trouble, obstacles, or hindrances in your way!

It's not that I've already reached the goal or have already completed the course. But I run to win that which Jesus Christ has already won for me. Brothers and sisters, I can't consider myself a winner yet. This is what I do: I don't look back, I lengthen my stride, and I run straight toward the goal to win the prize that God's heavenly call offers in Christ Jesus. (Philippians 3:12–14, GW)

This is the only race worth running. I've run hard right to the finish, believed all the way. (2 Timothy 4:7, MSG)

DAY 278

Pray the Word

Those who let God's Spirit lead them are the true children of God. His Spirit within us will never lead us wrong. We know to keep our eyes fixed on the Lord, but we need to keep our ears tuned into His still small voice.

The Holy Spirit will tell you who and what to pray for as you pray by the spirit with the Word of God. I spoke a prayer from Ephesians over my children and myself when they were young, and today as adults they continue to speak it over their own lives.

> *...that the God of our Lord Jesus Christ; the Father of glory, may give to you the spirit of wisdom and revelation in the knowledge of Him, the eyes of your understanding being enlightened; that you may know what is the hope of His calling, what are the riches of the glory of His inheritance in the saints, and what is the exceeding greatness of His power toward us who believe, according to the working of His mighty power which He worked in Christ when He raised him from the dead and seated Him at His right hand in heavenly places, far above all principality and power and might and dominion, and every name that is named, not only in this age but also in that which is to come.* (Ephesians 1:17–21, NKJV)

DAY 279

Praise Is Eternal

Now therefore, our God, We thank You and praise Your glorious name. (1 Chronicles 29:13, NKJV)

Every day, we need to be thankful and praise the Name of the Lord. This doesn't mean we have to give thanks for the not so good things that inevitably happen in our lives, but we should always be thankful for the Name of Jesus and the power in that Name. We know that the Lord has made each day for us, and so by choice we rejoice with thanksgiving!

One thing we will be doing throughout eternity is praising God. I'm so thankful that I get to enter His gates with joyful praise—today, tomorrow, and forever. We may leave this earth, but we will never leave His presence. He is eternally Emmanuel—God with us!

DAY 280

God-Made, Not Self-Made

Have you ever heard the term "self-made"? On yourdictionary.com it is defined as "something that is made by oneself or someone who has become successful through his own efforts,"[11] without God or anyone else.

God wants us to be successful in Him. He planned from the beginning that our success would arise through our connection to Him. God measures success differently than the world does. A self-made person may be successful in man's eyes, but not in God's.

Study this Book of Instruction continually. Meditate on it day and night so you will be sure to obey everything written in it. Only then will you prosper and succeed in all you do. (Joshua 1:8, NLT)

Be a God-made person rather than a self-made person. Only what we do for Christ will last.

DAY 281
He Is Always the Same

The weather and the seasons change, but our God never does. Living in Saskatchewan, one understands extreme changes in weather: one day it can be −30 degrees Celsius and the next +5. We can always rely on the Lord because He is our rock that cannot be moved. Circumstances may vary, the weather may change, and seasons may come and go, but He is the constant in our lives.

Put your trust in Him and you will never be disappointed. He is reliable and predictable, because He is always the same.

For Jesus doesn't change—yesterday, today, tomorrow, he's always totally himself. (Hebrews 13:8, MSG)

DAY 282

Jesus, Our Bridge over Troubled Water

During a praise night at church a song popped into my mind. I hadn't heard it since I was a child, and all I could remember was the title, "Bridge over Troubled Water," by Simon and Garfunkel. Thank God, Jesus is our bridge over troubled water. A suspension bridge sways as it is walked on, and many people fear crossing one. But there is no fear with the Lord, so just hold on as He walks with you. You will always be safe with Him.

Several years ago, in Wamena, Papua, Indonesia, I encountered a walking bridge over the river that went from the town to the jungle to get to the tribal villages. It was scary to walk on because it was made of planks that were broken, and had many missing pieces. God isn't like that—He is a place of safety because He connects us to heaven! Jesus is our mediator, who bridges the gap from Earth to Heaven and leads us away from troubled waters.

> *Jesus said to him, "I am the way, the truth, and the life. No one comes to the Father except through me." (John 14:6, NKJV)*

> *…There is one God and one Mediator who can reconcile God and humanity—the man Christ Jesus. (1 Timothy 2:5, NLT)*

DAY 283

The Rock on which We Stand

We can have great trust in someone, but no matter how incredible they are, at some time they are going to let us down. However, there is One whom we can completely trust! God will never disappoint us, because there is nothing but good in Him. He is one hundred percent trustworthy, faithful, and good! No matter what, we can count on God. He is our firm foundation through every storm!

Just thinking of my troubles and my lonely wandering makes me miserable. That's all I ever think about, and I am depressed. Then I remember something that fills me with hope. The Lord's kindness never fails! If he had not been merciful, we would have been destroyed. The Lord can always be trusted to show mercy each morning. Deep in my heart I say, "The Lord is all I need; I can depend on him!" (Lamentations 3:19–24, CEV)

DAY 284

In Times of Adversity

If you faint in the day of adversity, Your strength is small. (Proverbs 24:10, NKJV)

I was praying about a situation, and God spoke to me, "If you allow it, much good can come out of times of adversity." The Oxford Dictionary states that adversity means, "A difficult or unpleasant situation,"[12] and dictionary.com defines it as "...a condition marked by misfortune, calamity, or distress... an adverse or unfortunate event or circumstance."[13] The Bible tells us in the Book of James to *"...count it all joy when you fall into various trials"* (James 1:2, NKJV). We can count it all joy when we find ourselves in a difficult or unpleasant circumstance marked by misfortune, calamity, or distress.

When we "count it all joy," as the Word of God says, and let it rise up within us by the Holy Spirit, we will have the strength to endure any hardship. When adversity comes we should run into His arms, and His Joy will become our strength!

DAY 285

Healthy Choices

Through work, I participated in a training workshop called Healthy Start. The instructor talked about how we need to offer children food from all the food groups and make sure they are healthy food choices, but we are not responsible for making them eat. Our job is only to provide options, and the children choose whether they will eat them.

I know from experience that trying to force someone to eat something they dislike doesn't work. I remember having to sit for a long time at the table as a child because I wouldn't eat something. It only resulted in a power struggle between my parents and me. It caused much stress and tears, and it never obtained the desired results. I also attempted it with my own children, and it never worked.

Every day, God sets before us good spiritual food—healthy choices such as joy, peace, grace, mercy, and so much more. It is our decision whether we will eat what is set before us. How much we drink and eat of the things of His Spirit is up to us—our Father will never go against our will or get into a power struggle with us. We do our best to help the children understand the value of healthy eating, and in the same way, God shows us in His Word the benefits that will come to us through right choices.

> *Today I have given you the choice between death and life, between blessings and curses. Now I call on heaven and earth to witness the choice you make. Oh, that you would choose life, so that you and your descendants might live!* (Deuteronomy 30:19, NLT)

DAY 286

Our All-Consuming Fire

God is more than a Consuming Fire—He is our All-Consuming Fire. We often think of an all-consuming fire as being negative or destructive; however, a forest fire burns away all the dead undergrowth, allowing the forest to be renewed. What may appear to be negative or destructive is actually a good thing for the forest.

Some synonyms for "all-consuming" as stated on thesaurus.com are burning, blazing, eager, frenzied, heated, intense, passionate, red hot, and zealous.[14] The Lord wants to be so important in our lives that we are consumed with Him and can think of nothing else. When this happens, we will burn red hot with intensity, passion, and zeal that will purify, renew, and restore us, removing all distractions, hindrances, sins, and weights until it's all of Him and none of us.

Passion and zeal will either destroy or purify! The Lord is red-hot with zeal and passion for those who love and seek Him! He is not cool or lukewarm about anything. The Spirit of God is always burning with intensity and passion, so put on the cloak of zeal and let him be your All-Consuming Fire.

> *Do you see what we've got? An unshakable kingdom! And do you see how thankful we must be? Not only thankful, but brimming with worship, deeply reverent before God. For God is not an indifferent bystander. He's actively cleaning house, torching all that needs to burn, and he won't quit until it's all cleansed. God himself is Fire!*
> (Hebrews 12:28–29, MSG)

DAY 287

A Mere Reflection

We are merely a reflection of what is going on inside of us. If the inner man is being renewed every day, it will reflect on the outer man. We find ourselves saying things like, "What's wrong with that person? They are always miserable, never have anything good to say and are always angry." When we meet people like that, it's a reflection of a hard heart, just as addictions are a sign that there is something wrong on the inside. Before people are going to get free of these things, they need to have a change of heart.

There is only one way to freedom, one way to change the inner man—and that is through Jesus. We need to become a whole new person on the inside, and it will reflect on the outside. Does that mean we will completely change overnight? No, not likely. When you restore something like a house, the renovation process can make the house look worse at first, but the finished product is awesome. No one is beyond help: we are all a work in progress, and that's why we should never give up on anyone.

A gentle answer turns away rage, but a harsh word stirs up anger. (Proverbs 15:1, GW)

Patient persistence pierces through indifference; gentle speech breaks down rigid defences. (Proverbs 25:15, MSG)

DAY 288

Feed Your Inner Man

One morning as I was getting out of bed I got a cramp in my leg, so I prayed in Jesus' Name and it went away. There are several reasons for getting cramps: for example, your body might be lacking something like magnesium. When our physical bodies are lacking something, they don't function the way they should. A deficiency in iron can make us very tired, and a lack of certain oils can affect our mental wellbeing. We need to make sure that we're daily feeding our bodies everything they need to stay strong and healthy.

We also need to feed our inner man—our spirit—everything it needs to stay spiritually healthy and strong. Just as there are symptoms that tell us when our physical man is lacking something, there are symptoms that indicate things are lacking in our spiritual life. Have you ever heard the saying "A prayerless life is a powerless life"? If we don't spend time in the presence of the Lord, we will be become deficient in joy and have no spiritual strength. If we don't let the Prince of Peace rule and reign in our lives, we will lack peace. It isn't hard to see when someone is lacking spiritually: they have no freedom, no joy, and no peace. We need to take our spiritual vitamins, minerals, and oils every day: a healthy dose of prayer, worship and the Word of God.

The young lions lack and suffer hunger; But those who seek the Lord shall not lack any good thing. (Psalm 34:10, NKJV)

DAY 289

Tunnel Vision

In life we need to keep the main thing the main thing—and Jesus is the main thing. This song by Helen Howard Lemmel comes to mind:

> Turn your eyes upon Jesus,
> Look full in His wonderful face,
> And the things of earth will grow strangely dim,
> In the light of His glory and grace.

Tunnel vision is when a person cannot see to the right or left, but only straight ahead. It's like looking through a cylinder or a tunnel. As Christians, we need to have spiritual tunnel vision. The Bible tells us in James 1:8 (NKJV) that a *"double-minded man"* is *"unstable in all his ways."*

It's time to stop trying to see life from different perspectives and see through heaven's eyes. When we say someone has tunnel vision we're saying they are focused, single-minded, narrow-minded, or closed-minded. They have limited vision, and see from only one point of view. They have an extremely narrow outlook or a one-track mind; they are set on one thing. That is a good description of a person whose mind is focused on the Lord. We need to have a one-track mind so we see life only from God's perspective. Our thoughts need to become fixed on the Lord and things of eternal value.

> *And be constantly renewed in the spirit of your mind [having a fresh mental and spiritual attitude]...* (Ephesians 4:23, AMPC)

> *You have been raised to life with Christ, so set your hearts on the things that are in heaven, where Christ sits on the throne at the*

right side of God. Keep your mind fixed on things there, not on things here on earth. For you have died, and your life is hidden with Christ in God. (Colossians 3:1–3, GNT)

DAY 290

Catch the Big One

Winter is very cold, and sometimes we would like to just stay buried under a nice warm blanket and hibernate. However, we can't do that—we must keep going, adapt, and change with the seasons, both naturally and spiritually. We have to break out of our comfort zone and step into the new season. It can be a season of breakout where we break through all the rejection, doubts, fears, regrets, disappointments, and hurts that have crippled and held us back.

It's time to enter into a season of love, joy, peace, confidence, boldness, and unwavering trust and faith. It's harvest season, and we need to be like Peter; he fished all night and caught nothing, but at Jesus' word he let down his net.

It may seem like the wrong time or season to let down the net, but nevertheless we need to do it. We may have tried to make relationships right: we forgave, we prayed, we reached out to help, but nothing changed—but at the Lord's word, do it again. If we yield to Jesus like Simon Peter did, we will not only catch the big one that always seems to get away, but many others along with it.

But Simon answered and said to Him, "Master, we have toiled all night and caught nothing; nevertheless at Your word I will let down the net." (Luke 5:5, NKJV)

DAY 291

Keep Your Mind Fixed on God

...casting down arguments and every high thing that exalts itself against the knowledge of God, bringing every thought into captivity to the obedience of Christ... (2 Corinthians 10:5, NKJV)

We control what we think about. It's our choice to keep our minds fixed on the Lord. When we do, we find ourselves at peace because our trust and faith are in God. We aren't battling against people; ours is a spiritual battle, and it's fought in the mind. Our thoughts control our actions, so if someone isn't acting right, it's because they aren't meditating on the right things.

Right thinking will always produce positive actions. When we're having trouble trusting and have no peace, it's time to ask, "What am I focusing my mind on?" Wrong thoughts produce negative consequences, but right thinking produces positive outcomes. I know this to be true from my experience. This is the reason why people can have peace in a battle—because their minds aren't fixed on the circumstances, but on the One who calms the storm.

You will keep him in perfect peace, Whose mind is stayed on you...
(Isaiah 26:3a, NKJV)

DAY 292

The Battle Is in the Mind

Our battle is in the mind, and it is won or lost depending on how we choose to think. Every time we find ourselves in a storm, we must choose to keep our minds fixed on the Lord. We aren't fighting against people—rather, our battle is a spiritual one. If we will keep focused on God, we will be at peace and all will be well, no matter how the storm rages. When we allow our thoughts to rest on the circumstances rather than the Lord, we will not experience peace.

> *For though we walk in the flesh, we do not war according to the flesh. For the weapons of our warfare are not carnal but mighty in God for pulling down strongholds, casting down arguments and every high thing that exalts itself against the knowledge of God, bringing every thought into captivity to the obedience of Christ...*
> (2 Corinthians 10:3–5, NKJV)

DAY 293

God Is There in the Darkest Times

God is always with us, even in the darkest times of our lives. We can never escape from God. He is omnipresent! If we try to hide in the darkness, the light of His presence will always illuminate it. Even in the darkest times when all hell seems to have broken loose, and it feels like we're stumbling around in the dark and can't see anything but blackness, He is there. His light and glory will always overtake the darkness.

When God brought a plague of darkness on the land of Egypt, for three days it was so thick you could feel it. The people were in compete darkness, but where the Israelites lived there was light as usual, because light always overtakes darkness.

> *Is there anyplace I can go to avoid your Spirit? To be out of your sight?... Then I said to myself, "Oh, he even sees me in the dark! At night I'm immersed in the light!" It's a fact: darkness isn't dark to you; night and day, darkness and light, they're all the same to you.* (Psalm 139:7, 11–12, MSG)

No evil, difficulty, or trial can overcome us, because the light of the world shines from within us.

DAY 294

Faith to Walk on the Water

Prayer always makes my spirit excited because of the things God says and shows me. God has shown me that it's time to break out of my box, my comfort zone, and get zealous and passionate about living in extreme, unlimited Christianity. I've been provoked to develop a greater trust, confidence, and boldness in the Lord, and to do things I haven't done before.

Just like Peter, it's time for us to walk on the water. It's not natural for people to walk on water—this was a supernatural occurrence in Peter's life. He focused on Jesus, and walked in the supernatural by faith. As he kept his eyes on Jesus, he remained strong and the impossible became possible. We can walk in the supernatural power of God, experiencing signs, wonders, and miracles, as long as we stay focused on Jesus. Once Peter started looking at the waves, he lost faith and began to sink—the circumstances overwhelmed him.

> *And immediately Jesus stretched out His hand and caught him, and said to him, "O you of little faith, why did you doubt?"* (Matthew 14:31, NKJV)

Jesus said Peter had little faith because he began to doubt—yet walking on the water only required faith the size of a mustard seed. All we have to do is keep our eyes on the Lord, and we will have enough faith to walk in the supernatural.

DAY 295

No Storm Is Permanent

When the weather outside is nasty I would rather ignore it, but that's not possible. We have to go outside, even in storms. We can't ignore them or pretend that they don't exist. In a natural storm we put on our battle gear—hat, mitts, coat, boots—and carry on. Spiritually, we put on the armour of God and keep going, knowing that no storm is permanent.

> *For this reason, take up all the armor God supplies. Then you will be able to take a stand during these evil days. Once you have overcome all obstacles, you will be able to stand your ground.* (Ephesians 6:13, GW)

DAY 296

Rejoice, Pray, and be Thankful Always

Praise and worship should be a lifestyle—something we should be involved in on a continuous basis.

Rejoice always... (1 Thessalonians 5:16, NKJV)

Always means all the time! We have something to rejoice about all day long, because our names are written in the Lamb's Book of Life.

...pray continually... (1 Thessalonians 5:17, NIV)

"Continually" on dictionary.com is defined as "without cessation or intermission; unceasingly; always."[15] Prayer is just communicating with the Lord. We can be in continual communication with the Lord, no matter if we are at work, school, or home—even while sleeping. It is really about keeping our minds focused on God—being God-minded.

...give thanks in all circumstances; for this is God's will for you in Christ Jesus. (1 Thessalonians 5:18, NIV)

We don't thank God for the negative things that happen in our lives; rather, we are thankful for His help in times of trouble and for His grace and peace. We are thankful that with the Lord, we're able to get through any difficulty. He is always with us, so rejoice!

DAY 297

Arise and Shine

God very clearly says in His Word that everything has its time. There are different seasons for different things.

> *To everything there is a season, A time for every purpose under heaven...* (Ecclesiastes 3:1, NKJV)

God has been impressing upon my heart that the Church is moving into a season of unprecedented signs, wonders, and miracles like the world has never seen. Great things took place during the Book of Acts. There have been many great moves of God over history, but nothing like we are going to see in this coming season. It is a season of the impossible becoming possible. The glory of the Lord will be seen in the world; His glory will shine forth in the darkest regions of the earth, because light always overpowers darkness.

> *Arise, shine; For your light has come! And the glory of the Lord is risen upon you. For behold, the darkness shall cover the earth, and deep darkness the people; But the Lord will arise over you, and His glory will be seen upon you. The Gentiles shall come to your light, and kings to the brightness of your rising.*
>
> *Lift up your eyes all around, and see: They all gather together, they come to you; Your sons shall come from afar, and your daughters shall be nursed at your side. Then you shall see and become radiant, and your heart shall swell with joy...* (Isaiah 60:1–5a, NKJV)

DAY 298

Let Him Carry Your Burdens

Life can be difficult at times, and we should be careful how we think and react to circumstances that come our way. No one's life is void of bad circumstances; sometimes they are truly painful, but each of us needs to learn to make the choice to grow and push through the difficulties, realizing that because Jesus won, we win too!

He carried everything—absolutely everything—on the cross. You don't have to carry it, so cast all your sin, fear, regret, brokenness, grief, sorrow, sickness, and bitterness at the foot of the cross and let God carry it for you. In return, you will have a life filled with joy, hope, love, health, and freedom. We need to accept what Jesus has done for us and let Him carry our burdens.

He certainly has taken upon himself our suffering and carried our sorrows, but we thought God had wounded him, beat him, and punished him. He was wounded for our rebellious acts. He was crushed for our sins. He was punished so that we could have peace, and we received healing from his wounds. (Isaiah 53:4–5, GW)

DAY 299

The Key Is Positioning

When playing on a team, your positioning has a major effect on the outcome of the game. During the birthing process, a baby needs to drop into position for the birth to progress naturally. In the Church, God gives assignments to us individually and corporately, but for them to be fulfilled we need to be in position. We must position ourselves for victory!

David was in position to defeat Goliath, as were Gideon and his three hundred men in defeating the Midianite army. Spending time in God's presence positions us for victory. David did exactly that when looking after his father's sheep, and his times of worship positioned him to win the many battles he faced.

When we each do our part, the Church will be a mighty, unstoppable force that cannot be defeated. As we align our lives with God's plans and purposes, the things we have dreamed about and desired to see happen will come to pass.

> *For I know the plans that I have for you, says the Lord, plans for peace and not for evil, to give you a future and a hope.* (Jeremiah 29:11, MEV)

> *Trust in the Lord with all your heart, And lean not on your own understanding; In all your ways acknowledge Him, and He shall direct your paths.* (Proverbs 3:5–6, NKJV)

DAY 300

Simplify and Intensify

Recently, God spoke to my heart, telling me that it was time to both simplify and intensify at the same time. We simplify by disengaging from unnecessary things that take attention away from the Kingdom of God. When I think of the word "intensify," stronger and extreme come to mind.

Simplifying and intensifying mean ridding our lives of distractions to enable us to be more focused and single-minded in our relationship with the Lord. We need to be passionate and cloaked in zeal in our pursuit of God, causing us to go deeper in Him. It's time for extraordinary and uncommon supernatural occurrences to become the norm. When we simplify and intensify, we are positioned to model and demonstrate the power of God in our everyday life.

And from the days of John the Baptist until the present time, the kingdom of heaven has endured violent assault, and violent men seize it by force [as a precious prize—a share in the heavenly kingdom is sought with most ardent zeal and intense exertion]. (Matthew 11:12, AMPC)

DAY 301

Becoming Consumed

Our minds become fixed or focused when we are consumed with something or someone. For example, when we start dating we find ourselves thinking about that person continually and we become consumed with thoughts of them. We just can't get enough of their presence.

We can be that consumed and focused on doing God's will and pleasing Him too. This doesn't mean that we neglect our families or jobs, but God becomes our number one priority. When we put the Lord first, we position ourselves for success and victory. Our life doesn't become free of difficulties or challenges, but we are enabled to go through troubled waters victoriously.

David was a man after God's own heart, consumed with passion for the Lord, yet when he got his focus on the wrong things he made some huge mistakes. It's not about our strength in the Lord, it's that we need to keep our attention on Him. Otherwise we will set our eyes on the wrong things, just like David did. Troubles happen, but those of our own making can be avoided if we will stay consumed with the Lord. Jesus is our example, and He was full of passion for God's house.

His disciples remembered that it was written, "Zeal for your house will consume Me." (John 2:17, MEV)

DAY 302

Fix Your Mind on Right Things

We need to learn not to worry, but to ask God for what we need with thanksgiving. We will be filled with joy and peace, having our hearts and minds guarded through Christ Jesus so we can pray effectively.

When our minds are focused on negative things, we won't rejoice or be thankful; our thoughts will be anxious and fearful. We need to take care of what we allow our hearts and minds to dwell on. We should always be God-conscious, fixing our mind on right things so we will be full of joy and thanksgiving.

In conclusion, my friends, fill your minds with those things that are good and that deserve praise: things that are true, noble, right, pure, lovely, and honorable. (Philippians 4:8, GNT)

DAY 303

Soar Like an Eagle

It is time for believers to soar like eagles to new heights above every negative situation and difficulty. We should see ourselves seated with the Lord, high above every circumstance of our life. We can develop spiritual insight that enables us to see beyond the earthly realm into heavenly places, with keen eyesight like an eagle. We can see to a greater measure as we soar higher in God's presence, in the same way John did on the island of Patmos!

> *I was in the Spirit on the Lord's Day, and I heard behind me a loud voice, as of a trumpet, saying, "I am the Alpha and Omega, the First and the Last," and, "What you see, write in a book…"* (Revelation 1:10–11a, NKJV)

DAY 304
New Heights

It's time to fearlessly leave our place of comfort, knowing that God is always with us. When ready, eagles push their young out of the nest, which forces them to learn to fly. The father will swoop down under the eaglet to carry it if it falters.

If we fall, we don't need to worry because our Heavenly Father will carry us until we're ready to soar again. One of the best ways to learn to soar to heavenly places in Him is to spend time in worship. It will take you out of this earthly realm and into the heavenly one.

Like an eagle teaching its young to fly, catching them safely on its spreading wings, the Lord kept Israel from falling. (Deuteronomy 32:11, GNT)

DAY 305

Reach Out in Love

There is a group of people whom we have failed—they have been robbed, beaten up, stolen from, and left for dead in their sin with no hope. But I believe that it's turnaround time for them! God hasn't forgotten those who have been bruised, brokenhearted, rejected, and hated—and He will never fail them. The story of the Good Samaritan is a great example for us to live by. We need to show God's love and compassion to hurting people.

> So he answered and said, "'You shall love the Lord your God with all your heart, with all your soul, with all your strength, and with all your mind,' and 'your neighbor as yourself.'" (Luke 10:27, NKJV)

The religious leaders in the story of the Good Samaritan knew God's law, but they didn't have a revelation of its meaning. They were afraid to get involved, and cared more about their own safety than helping others. The Good Samaritan understood what it was like to be an outcast, so he couldn't ignore the man on the side of the road.

When we choose to reach out and get involved in people's lives, we're letting the love of God shine through us by the Holy Spirit. In essence, we are being Jesus' hands and feet. The Holy Spirit lives within us and has anointed us to bring healing. All we have to do is reach out in love and God will do the rest.

DAY 306

Show Compassion

The Good Samaritan chose to reach out in love. He had compassion on the injured man, so he chose to help. He poured oil and wine onto his wounds—liquids that are often representative of the Holy Spirit.

> *This hope does not disappoint us, for God has poured out his love into our hearts by means of the Holy Spirit, who is God's gift to us.* (Romans 5:5, GNT)

God has anointed us to heal the brokenhearted, binding up their wounds. The Good Samaritan didn't just bind up the robbed man's wounds and leave him on the road. He brought him to the inn where he could be further cared for. He gave not only of his time to get him there, but his resources and his money to help him.

We need to be willing to give up our time, resources, and even money to reach out with compassion to those on whom society has given up. We should be ready to receive society's outcasts. They will rise out of the ashes and darkness and come into His marvellous light if we will reach out to them with God's love and compassion.

> *He heals the brokenhearted and binds up their wounds.* (Psalm 147:3, NKJV)

DAY 307

It's Time for His House to Be Full

Society's outcasts will not come to us—we have to go after them and offer them a compelling reason to come in. This is what happened in the parable of the man who invited many to a great feast. Those who were invited all had excuses why they could not come.

> *The servant went back and told all this to his master. The master was furious and said to his servant, "Hurry out to the streets and alleys of the town, and bring back the poor, the crippled, the blind, and the lame." Soon the servant said, "Your order has been carried out, sir, but there is room for more." So the master said to the servant, "Go out to the country roads and lanes and make people come in, so that my house will be full."* (Luke 14:21–23, GNT)

It is time for God's house to be full, but it's not going to look like many think it will. It's going to become a mighty army, an unstoppable force in the earth, just like David's mighty men were. They started out as a group of people who were distressed, in debt, and discontented, but they became the powerful warriors of their king.

DAY 308

No Breakthrough until We Pray Through

There will be no breakthrough until God's people learn to pray through. We need to simplify yet intensify our lives. We need to live a more simple life by getting rid of things that complicate and cause distractions. We need to clean house, to make room in our lives for what is important.

We need to position ourselves for breakthrough and victory. That position is a posture of prayer. We need to intensify our prayer lives. Be persistent: grab onto the horns of the altar and don't let go until there is a breakthrough—even if it means praying all night. We need to keep walking around the walls with prayer until they fall. There are people who won't return to the Lord or get free or get their breakthrough until we pray through to victory. We need to be like the widow who just kept going back to the unjust judge until he avenged her.

Even he rendered a just decision in the end. So don't you think God will surely give justice to his chosen people who cry out to him day and night? Will he keep putting them off? I tell you, he will grant justice to them quickly! (Luke 18:7–8a, NLT)

DAY 309

Let His River Flow

The river of God flows out of our mouths as we praise and lift up the Name of Jesus. Wherever the river flows, everything lives. Water cleanses, purifies, washes, refreshes, restores, and causes things to grow and germinate: it causes things that are dormant to take root, and things that seem dead to come to life once again. Nothing can live without water. We need to learn to get into God's presence and let the river flow, and everything that the river touches will live.

> *In my vision, the man brought me back to the entrance of the Temple. There I saw a stream flowing east from beneath the door of the Temple and passing to the right of the altar on its south side....*
>
> *Then he said to me, "This river flows through the desert into the valley of the Dead Sea. The waters of this stream will make the salty waters of the Dead Sea fresh and pure. There will be swarms of living things wherever the water of this river flows. Fish will abound in the Dead Sea, for its waters will become fresh. Life will flourish wherever this water flows."* (Ezekiel 47:1, 8–9, NLT)

DAY 310

Heaven on Earth

I was thinking about my husband, who passed away from this earthly life to the heavenly life, and about how amazing it would be if I was able to experience what he is living right now. Then I thought, "That *is* what God wants us to experience right now—heaven on earth." He wants us to draw so close to Him that we really experience sitting in heavenly places with Him. We can go deeper and higher than we could ever imagine!

Enoch walked with God, and he was no more. He got so close to God that he just walked into eternity without physically dying. It's not that God is going to take us to heaven that way, but through Him, we can have faith like Enoch had to go places where we have never gone before. This will bring much pleasure to God. He so desires to be with us. Faith pleases God!

Jesus is coming back again, and if we are still living on this earth when He returns, like Enoch we will be taken to heaven without seeing death. Why? God is well pleased with us if we have accepted His gift of salvation. My husband Clarence received that free gift of eternal life in 1985, and is now forever with the Lord. Faith pleases God—faith in what Jesus did for us, and believing and receiving that gift. It puts us in right standing with God, and that pleases Him.

> *It was faith that kept Enoch from dying. Instead, he was taken up to God, and nobody could find him, because God had taken him up. The scripture says that before Enoch was taken up, he had pleased God.* (Hebrews 11:5, GNT)

DAY 311

The Missing Link

The book of Acts is a record of the start of the church age, and it was a very exciting time. It was the beginning of the outpouring of the Holy Spirit on all people, and many were saved. There were continual conversions, miracles, and signs and wonders throughout the Book of Acts. It was not just a onetime thing that happened on the day of Pentecost.

While spending time reading through Acts, I asked myself, "Why aren't we seeing these things on a continual basis today?" The Spirit is the missing link, and we need to be filled daily with Him. It's more than just having someone lay hands on us and being inspired to pray in the Spirit. That is only the beginning.

Later, after the initial baptism with the Holy Spirit, the Bible says that believers were baptized with the Holy Spirit and Fire. If we have been baptized in the Holy Spirit, why would we need to be baptized with the Holy Spirit and Fire? Because we need to be continually infused with the Power of the Holy Spirit. When Jesus was baptized in the Jordan River, He was filled with the Spirit, but when He came out of the wilderness, He came out in the Power of the Holy Spirit.

We need to go daily to God's fuelling station and get our tank filled. It is the fuel that fires up our engines. If we don't fill up on the Holy Spirit, we will run out of power. If we are to operate in signs, wonders, and miracles, doing even greater works than what Jesus did, we must be anointed with the Holy Spirit and Power!

> *...how God anointed Jesus of Nazareth with the Holy Spirit and with power, who went about doing good and healing all who were oppressed by the devil, for God was with Him.* (Acts 10:38, NKJV)

DAY 312

He Is Restoring What Has Been Stolen

One morning I woke up and heard, "The Lord is restoring what the locust has stolen." The book of Joel says that God will give us the former and the latter rain, plenty of grain, and vats overflowing with wine and oil. It also says that He will restore what has been lost and what the locusts have stolen. The Lord is sending the former and the latter rain, and the Word of God will abound and the Holy Spirit will begin to overflow into people's lives.

> *Afterward I will pour out my Spirit on everyone: your sons and daughters will proclaim my message; your old people will have dreams, and your young people will see visions. At that time I will pour out my Spirit even on servants, both men and women.* (Joel 2:28–29, GNT)

God is in the restoration business, and He is restoring what the enemy has stolen. Every time He pours out His Spirit, He restores, and every time He restores, His Spirit flows!

DAY 313

Never Give Up

Even though we would like time to stand still, it continues to move forward. In the race of life, we move forward consistently. We can't ever change the past or turn back the hands of time, but we can affect what happens in the future with our prayers.

Prayer changes our future, so never give up. Be like the widow who kept going to the unjust judge until she received justice. Go after those things that seem impossible, forgotten, or lost—God will restore all to you. Never write yourself or anyone else off. Be persistent: never quit or give up in prayer!

> *Make this your common practice: Confess your sins to each other and pray for each other so that you can live together whole and healed. The prayer of a person living right with God is something powerful to be reckoned with. Elijah, for instance, human just like us, prayed hard that it wouldn't rain, and it didn't—not a drop for three and a half years. Then he prayed that it would rain, and it did. The showers came and everything started growing again.*
>
> *My dear friends, if you know people who have wandered off from God's truth, don't write them off. Go after them. Get them back and you will have rescued precious lives from destruction and prevented an epidemic of wandering away from God.* (James 5:16–20, MSG)

DAY 314

He Is a God for Today

I am so thankful that God never changes—He is one hundred percent reliable. If He answered prayer yesterday, it's guaranteed that He will answer today and tomorrow. Jesus is our Prince of Peace, our provider, and many other things—today, tomorrow, and forever.

Most importantly, He is our God for today. What do you need today? Peace, joy, forgiveness, wisdom, direction, or provision? It's here for the taking, like fresh manna from heaven. It's not yesterday's leftovers, but a daily smorgasbord.

> *But seek first the kingdom of God and His righteousness, and all these things shall be added to you.* (Matthew 6:33, NKJV)

God is the Lord of today, not just yesterday or tomorrow. He cares about our today and is ready to help us now!

> *Give your entire attention to what God is doing right now, and don't get worked up about what may or may not happen tomorrow. God will help you deal with whatever hard things come up when the time comes.* (Matthew 6:34, MSG)

DAY 315

Speak and Believe

Declaring and believing what the scriptures say is very powerful!

And Jesus answered them, Truly I say to you, if you have faith (a firm relying trust) and do not doubt, you will not only do what has been done to the fig tree, but even if you say to this mountain, Be taken up and cast into the sea, it will be done. (Matthew 21:21, AMPC)

Death and life are in the power of the tongue, and those who love it will eat its fruit. (Proverbs 18:21, NKJV)

We have the God-given ability to speak to the dead places in our lives and watch them be resurrected. By our words, we can also curse negative things and watch them die. Jesus spoke to the fig tree in Matthew 21 and it withered up and died. We declare to the dead and broken places "Arise," and because we believe, we will receive.

DAY 316

The Power of the Tongue

Death and life are in the power of the tongue... (Proverbs 18:1a, NKJV)

We really have been given power through our tongue to determine death and life. Jesus cursed a fig tree because there was no fruit on it. He said it would never produce fruit again, and it withered up and died. What we say makes all the difference! We need to speak to those things in our lives that are not producing fruit.

Jesus said in Mark 11 that if we would believe and not doubt, we could do much more than what He did. He said we could speak to mountains and they would move. We need to speak to the hindrances and obstacles in our lives such as fear, anxiety, depression, worry, unforgiveness, feelings of rejection, thoughts of inadequacy, anger, addictions, and physical and mental illnesses. There is power in the words we speak and pray. Our tongues really do have the power to declare life or death—the choice is ours!

I call heaven and earth as witnesses today against you, that I have set before you life and death, blessing and cursing; therefore choose life, that both you and your descendants may live... (Deuteronomy 30:19, NKJV)

DAY 317

Living Waters

One day while driving in my car, these words rose up in me spontaneously and I began singing them:

Rivers of living water,
Rivers of living water,
Rivers of living water flow through me.
Living waters restore and make me whole.

Restoration and wholeness remind me of the story of Naaman in the Bible. When Naaman obeyed Elisha and dipped himself in the muddy Jordan River, it became to him a river of living water—of healing and restoration. Even though Naaman wasn't an Israelite, he was healed. The river of God is for all who choose to jump in. It will restore our lives and make us clean.

> *So he did it. He went down and immersed himself in the Jordan seven times, following the orders of the Holy Man. His skin was healed; it was like the skin of a little baby. He was as good as new.* (2 Kings 5:14, MSG)

> *…and everything will live wherever the river goes.* (Ezekiel 47:9b, NKJV)

DAY 318

It Isn't a One-Time Thing

In the story of Naaman, he didn't just dip his body in the Jordan River once, but *seven* times, as he was instructed to do. Getting into the river of God's presence shouldn't be a one-time event, but a daily occurrence. We need to press in until we receive from God. Naaman had to choose to trust and obey, and when he did, he received his healing.

> *So he went down and dipped himself in the Jordan seven times, according to the word of the man of God, and his flesh returned like the flesh of a little boy, and he was clean.* (2 Kings 5:14, MEV)

DAY 319

Uniquely Gifted

Not one of us is alike—we are all uniquely gifted. Even though people may have the same motivational gifts (see Romans 12:6–8), they have unique combinations that make them different from anyone else. If each of us were to bake a cake, we may all have the same ingredients, but every recipe is different and we would have varying amounts of each ingredient. One recipe would call for two cups of flour and another only one cup, giving each cake its own unique texture and taste.

My main motivational gift is exhortation, but I also have the gifts of mercy and giving, and the combination of these gifts colours the way I think. Be thankful for who God made you to be, and be your best for Him. We can confidently follow the plan God has for our lives, knowing that He has gifted us accordingly. It will be a plan that fits with our gifts.

> *For I know the plans that I have for you, says the Lord, plans for peace and not for evil, to give you a future and a hope.* (Jeremiah 29:11, MEV)

DAY 320

We Are Well Able

God is on the move, and His people are rising up to do His will! I believe it's time for the Church to do great things for God! The wind of His Spirit is blowing, the fire is being kindled, and the river of God is flowing. His Spirit is flowing from us—His Living Temples—into a dry and thirsty land, resulting in changed lives.

Repentance and righteousness will become the norm. People will come to Jesus, the Living Water, where they will be cleansed, purified, renewed, refreshed, and restored, abounding with new life. This will happen when we allow God's Spirit to flow out of us, unhindered by negativity and unbelief and with hearts full of thanksgiving and praise. We need to be like Caleb and Joshua when they said, "We are capable; we can do this," in spite of the negative report of the other spies.

Then Caleb quieted the people before Moses, and said, "Let us go up at once and take possession, for we are well able to overcome it."
But the men who had gone up with him said, "We are not able to go up against the people, for they are stronger than we."
(Numbers 13:30–31, NKJV)

We are well able when we obey His Holy Spirit, so whose report will we choose to believe?

DAY 321

The Importance of What We Think On

What we allow our thoughts to dwell on is so important. Our thoughts produce the words we speak and write. Our thoughts come from our inner self, the Spirit of God, or the enemy of our souls, and produce what we say and do. If our minds are fixed on positive things, the words we write, speak, and act will be encouraging, uplifting, and faith-building to others. If our minds are set on negative thoughts, the words we write, speak, and act will be discouraging, hopeless, unbelieving, and faith-killing.

> *My son, pay attention to my words. Bend your ear to my speech. Don't let them slip from your sight. Guard them in your mind. They are life to those who find them, and healing for their entire body. More than anything you guard, protect your mind, for life flows from it. Have nothing to do with a corrupt mouth; keep devious lips far from you. Focus your eyes straight ahead; keep your gaze on what is in front of you. Watch your feet on the way, and all your paths will be secure. Don't deviate a bit to the right or the left; turn your feet away from evil.* (Proverbs 4:20–27, CEB)

DAY 322

Overwhelmed

Have you ever been overwhelmed by the presence of God? Recently, at the end of the workday I was overwhelmed by His amazing presence. It felt like a little piece of heaven had settled over my office.

God is always with us, but His presence overwhelms us at times when we aren't expecting it. We live in continual communication with God, yet it is special when He visits us unexpectedly. It's like getting a surprise visit, and we are excited and overwhelmed by it. God's love, joy, and peace are overwhelming. There is rest and restoration in His presence for the weary and broken-hearted.

You will show me the path of life; In Your presence is fullness of joy; At your right hand are pleasures forevermore. (Psalm 16:11, NKJV)

Surely the righteous shall give thanks to Your name; The upright shall dwell in Your presence. (Psalm 140:13, NKJV)

God longs to visit us and to overwhelm us with His very presence. We just need to take the time to visit with Him.

DAY 323

Resurrection Time

Wherever God's presence is, His glory flows like a river, bringing restoration to us. God wants to restore everything the enemy has stolen, killed, or destroyed. It's resurrection time! It's time for those dead bones to rise.

> *God rises up and scatters his enemies. Those who hate him run away in defeat. As smoke is blown away, so he drives them off; as wax melts in front of the fire, so do the wicked perish in God's presence. But the righteous are glad and rejoice in his presence; they are happy and shout for joy.*
>
> *Sing to God, sing praises to his name; prepare a way for him who rides on the clouds. His name is the Lord—be glad in his presence!*
>
> *God, who lives in his sacred Temple, cares for orphans and protects widows. He gives the lonely a home to live in and leads prisoners out into happy freedom, but rebels will have to live in a desolate land.*
>
> *O God, when you led your people, when you marched across the desert, the earth shook, and the sky poured down rain, because of the coming of the God of Sinai, the coming of the God of Israel. You caused abundant rain to fall and restored your worn-out land…*
> (Psalm 68:1–9, GNT)

DAY 324

It's Restoration Time for the Church

Arise, shine; For your light has come! And the glory of the Lord has risen upon you. For behold, the darkness shall cover the earth, and deep darkness the people; But the Lord will arise over you, And His glory will be seen upon you. (Isaiah 60:1–2, NKJV)

As I was praying one day, a thought came to me: "The glory of the Lord will be seen upon the Church as it is restored to a place of prominence, respect, and authority in society." This word is for the Body of Christ and not just for specific denominations or groups. As we unite together as city, regional, and national churches, we will see restoration come to the whole Body of Christ.

The Bible gives us a different view of the Church—we think locally or denominationally, but for example, the churches of Ephesus were called the *Church* of Ephesus. It's been said that the Church is outdated and irrelevant for today, but that's not true. The enemy has lied and caused much mistrust in society towards the Church. That is subject to change, because God is healing and restoring the Church.

Zion is often symbolic of the Church. Jeremiah 30 speaks of the restoration and healing of Judah and Israel, but it's prophetic to the Church of today.

The time is coming, declares the Lord, when I will bring back my people Israel and Judah from captivity, says the Lord....

I will restore your health, and I will heal your wounds, declares the Lord, because you were labeled an outcast, "Zion, the lost cause." ...

There will be laughter and songs of thanks. I will add to their numbers so they don't dwindle away. I will honor them so they aren't humiliated. Their children will thrive as they did long ago, and their community will be established before me. I will punish their oppressors. (Jeremiah 30:3, 17, 19–20, CEB)

Praise the Lord! For it is good to sing praises to our God; For it is pleasant, and praise is beautiful.

The Lord builds up Jerusalem; He gathers together the outcasts of Israel. He heals the brokenhearted and binds up their wounds. (Psalm 147:1–3, NKJV)

DAY 325

Addicted to God

We are always going to have to fight against discouragement and discontentment in our lives. Recently I had a sense of both trying to invade my life, and I wondered what was wrong with me. I had been pressing into God's presence, so I figured this shouldn't have been happening. I usually see the good in negative situations and have learned to praise my way through anything. God's joy really is our strength!

I realized that the more we press into God's presence, the more we need to continue seeking Him. It's exactly when we feel less than our best that we need more of God's presence. Otherwise we will find ourselves getting down and allowing wrong thoughts to invade our minds. Maybe we haven't stopped praying, worshipping, or spending time with the Lord, but we always need more of Him. Enough is never enough—we need the Lord more and more! He is very addicting—in a good way. Any time negativity strikes, be thankful and worship God, and rivers of Living Water will flow, bringing restoration to your soul!

> *Why am you discouraged, my soul? Why are you so restless? Put your hope in God, because I will still praise him. He is my savior and my God.* (Psalm 42:5, GW)

DAY 326

Let Your Light Shine

There are things that we can try to put off to the next day, such as shovelling snow after a storm, but we should never put off praying or going to church. Ultimately, procrastination is never a good thing for us. Storms in life come up suddenly, and the only way to get through is by riding them out with the Lord. He is the Way-Maker through any storm, because He is a beacon of light showing us the way.

It's time for the Church to arise and shine. The local church is really the people that gather, and not the building. We come together, letting our lights shine brighter, so the world will see Jesus. The world and its people are in great darkness, but the Lord has risen over us, and His glory shines upon us His church.

One single light shining will disperse the darkness around us, but many lights shining together will cause the darkness to vanish. Jesus is the Light of the World, and the Church should shine forth His light for all to see.

> *You are like light for the whole world. A city built on a hill cannot be hidden. No one lights a lamp and puts it under a bowl; instead it is put on the lampstand, where it gives light for everyone in the house. In the same way your light must shine before people, so that they will see the good things you do and praise your Father in heaven.* (Matthew 5:14–16, GNT)

DAY 327

Don't Doubt What God Shows You

We shouldn't ever doubt what God shows us. Sometimes we doubt or second-guess when God shows us things through dreams, visions, prophetic utterances, or revelations that rise up out of our spirit. We need to learn to trust what God shows or tells us in the light of His presence. John 4:24 tells us that God is Spirit, and we must worship Him in spirit and in truth. When we draw close to the Lord, we will see into the realm of the Spirit more. We communicate with the Lord through our spirit; we have a soul made up of our mind, will, and emotions; and we are housed in a body.

The Holy Spirit resides in us, so it shouldn't seem strange when God communicates through dreams, visions, prophetic utterances, and spiritual gifts. When we communicate with the Lord and allow our spirits to rule, we will hear and see more clearly.

Joel prophetically declared our era and Peter preached about it on the day of Pentecost. Through daily communication with the Holy Spirit, we will declare what God is saying through others as well. God longs to relate with us, Spirit to spirit. On the island of Patmos, God showed John what is and what is to come. As the world gets darker, our spirits need to shine brighter. He wants to pour His Spirit out on us, so that His Spirit will flow in, through, and out of us into a dark world.

> *But this is what was spoken by the prophet Joel: "And it shall come to pass in the last days, says God, That I will pour out of My Spirit on all flesh; Your sons and your daughters shall prophesy, Your young men shall see visions, Your old men shall dream dreams. And on My*

> *menservants and on My maidservants I will pour out My Spirit in those days; and they shall prophesy."* (Acts 2:16–18, NKJV)

These are those days, so don't doubt in the dark what God has shown you in the light.

DAY 328

What Are You Allowing?

What we allow into our minds and our bodies is important. If we continually feed our bodies the wrong things, they will become overloaded with toxins. One of the best ways to remove toxins from our bodies is to drink plenty of water, because it cleanses, purifies, refreshes, and restores. In our bodies, the water we take in is like a river carrying nutrients to our cells, helping with digestion, removing toxins, and keeping our organs functioning normally.

Our minds can become toxic as well when we allow wrong thoughts to grow. We need the water of the Spirit to cleanse, purify, refresh, and restore our minds. Our minds are washed clean of wrong thoughts by the Holy Spirit and through meditating on the Word of God.

Christ used the word to make the church clean by washing it with water. (Ephesians 5:26b, NCV)

Finally, brethren, whatever things are true, whatever things are noble, whatever things are just, whatever things are pure, whatever things are lovely, whatever things are of good report, if there is any virtue and if there is anything praiseworthy—meditate on these things. (Philippians 4:8, NKJV)

DAY 329

Get Wisdom

The Bible talks about the seven pillars of wisdom in Proverbs chapter nine. According to Christian neuroscientist Dr. Caroline Leaf, our brain is divided into seven pillars of thought, which are the seven different ways that we think or process information. Dr. Leaf says in her book, *The Gift in You*, that "You have an amazing gift, a unique and special way of thinking, so you see the world from a different perspective."[16] We use all seven pillars of thought, but certain pillars dominant our thinking process. If the dominant way you think is "linguistic," you will process thoughts first with written and spoken words, then go through all the other pillars with every thought.

The mind is an amazing thing! When we think right thoughts and think about positive things, we will grow in wisdom and understanding. However; if our thinking is wrong, we'll lack wisdom and understanding and our thoughts will become toxic and negative.

> *Listen, friends, to some fatherly advice; sit up and take notice so you'll know how to live. I'm giving you good counsel; don't let it go in one ear and out the other.* (Proverbs 4:1–2, MSG)

> *Get wisdom! Get understanding! Do not forget, nor turn away from the words of my mouth. Do not forsake her, and she will preserve you; Love her, and she will keep you.* (Proverbs 4:5–6, NKJV)

> *The beginning of wisdom: Get wisdom! Get understanding before anything else. Highly esteem her, and she will exalt you. She will honor you if you will embrace her. She will place a graceful wreath on your head; she will give you a glorious crown.*

Listen, my son, and take in my speech, then the years of your life will be many. I teach you the path of wisdom. I lead you in straight courses. When you walk, you won't be hindered; when you run, you won't stumble. Hold onto instruction; don't slack off; protect it, for it is your life... The way of the righteous is like morning light that gets brighter and brighter till it is full day. The path of the wicked is like deep darkness; they don't know where they will stumble.
My son, pay attention to my words. Bend your ear to my speech. Don't let them slip from your sight. Guard them in your mind. They are life to those who find them, and healing for their entire body. (Proverbs 4:7–13, 18–22, CEB)

Be careful how you think; your life is shaped by your thoughts. Never say anything that isn't true. Have nothing to do with lies and misleading words. (Proverbs 4:23–24, GNT)

Let your eyes look straight ahead and your sight be focused in front of you. Carefully walk a straight path, and all your ways will be secure. Do not lean to the right or to the left. Walk away from evil. (Proverbs 4:25–27, GW)

DAY 330

My Destiny Is in My Hands

Recently this thought came to mind: "My destiny and future are in my hands, not God's." I've often heard the opposite: "My future is in God's hands." God does have a specific plan and purpose for each one of us, but we determine whether it will come to pass. God has predetermined our destiny, but it's our choice to walk in it.

Moses was destined to lead the Israelites out of slavery in Egypt, but he still had to choose to obey and follow God's instructions. God's plan and purpose for Queen Esther was to save her people from being killed, but she had to do what her uncle Mordecai asked, and go to the king uninvited. It was God's will that Esther seek help from the king and go before him without being summoned, but it was still her choice to make.

> *For if you remain completely silent at this time, relief and deliverance will arise for the Jews from another place, but you and your father's house will perish. Yet who knows whether you have come to the kingdom for such a time as this?* (Esther 4:14, NKJV)

DAY 331

God Has a Plan, a Destiny

For I know the plans that I have for you, says the Lord, plans for peace and not for evil, to give you a future and a hope. (Jeremiah 29:11, MEV)

God has a great plan and a wonderful destiny for each one of us—a plan filled with good and not evil, a future filled with hope! It is, however, our choice to walk in it. It is God's will for all men to repent and receive salvation that comes through Jesus Christ, but it is always a choice. It was God the Father's predetermined will for Jesus to go to the cross, but it was still His choice to make.

Father, if it is Your will, take this cup away from Me; nevertheless not My will, but Yours, be done. (Luke 22:42, NKJV)

No matter what God's plan is for us, He will never take away our free will to choose. Just because something is predetermined doesn't mean it will happen—it's always our choice.

...having predestined us to adoption as sons by Jesus Christ to Himself, according to the good pleasure of His will... (Ephesians 1:5, NKJV)

Your destiny is in your hands!

DAY 332

Living an Extraordinary Life

God has an incredible plan for each one of our lives, but we must choose to walk in it.

> *Trust in the Lord with all your heart, And lean not on your own understanding; In all your ways acknowledge Him, And He shall direct your paths.* (Proverbs 3:5–6, NKJV)

God really does want us to live an extraordinary life, but we have to choose to believe that we can really live that way. John Bevere says in his book *Extraordinary: The Life You're Meant to Live*:

> The truth is, God not only desires for you to live extraordinary but has equipped you to do so. Don't ever forget these words. Etch them on the tablet of your heart. A remarkable, amazing, extraordinary life is not restricted to certain individuals or professions. It doesn't matter who you are or how you serve in life. If you're a schoolteacher, businessperson, government leader, stay-at-home-mom, athlete, factory worker, hairstylist, student, pastor (the list is endless), it doesn't matter because you were created for extraordinary achievements in that role. The power to accomplish remarkable feats and live an exceptional life is not tied to an occupation but to a disposition of the heart. This is not only God's will but also His great pleasure.[17]

We need to say "Yes, Lord—not my will but Yours." His will is for us to demonstrate His glory and power, with and for the Lord, through supernatural, extraordinary signs and wonders.

DAY 333

Worship Is a Lifestyle

As believers in Christ, it is important that we spend time individually and corporately in God's presence through prayer, praise, and worship. We should corporately spend time with members of our own churches, but also with other churches in our communities. Praying, praising, and worshipping are all ways of communing with the Father, Son, and Holy Spirit. We are encouraged in Scripture to do this all the time—it should be a way of life. When we rise in the morning or when we go to sleep at night, declarations of thanksgiving and praise should be in our mouths and on our lips.

I have learned from experience that we are well able to praise our way through any trouble. Praise and worship will bring you through the courtyard and into the very throne room of the king. Praise isn't just for the midnight hour. I am very confident in saying this: Paul and Silas had to have cultivated a lifestyle of praise to be able to act on it during the midnight hour. Worship was their lifestyle!

Rejoice always, pray continually... (1 Thessalonians 5:16–17, NIV)

DAY 334

Who Dominates Your Thinking?

How does a person get to a place of hopelessness in their life? I have thought about and studied this problem, and personally have seen people come to such a place. I believe it has much to do with our thought life—what we meditate on and allow to enter our minds. It is a spiritual battle. Who is going to dominate our thinking—the enemy, or the Spirit of God?

We need to constantly fill our minds with thoughts of God. We do this by continually rejoicing and thanking the Lord with our prayers and praises. When our minds are continually fixed on Him, there is no room for wrong thoughts.

> *Rejoice always, pray continually, give thanks in all circumstances; for this is God's will for you in Christ Jesus.* (1 Thessalonians 5:16–18, NIV)

> *Therefore by Him let us continually offer the sacrifice of praise to God, that is, the fruit of our lips, giving thanks to His name.* (Hebrews 13:15, NKJV)

When you choose to rejoice, pray, be thankful, and praise continually, your thinking will be right and you won't become depressed or hopeless.

DAY 335

Train Yourself to Think Right

We must train ourselves to think God's way. We are positive by nature because we are made in the image of God and He is only positive; there is nothing negative about Him. With the help of the enemy of our souls, we learn to think incorrectly.

Our thoughts become our attitudes and actions, so if we think according to the Word of God, we won't act negatively. When we train ourselves to think right by meditating on God's Word, it prevents us from coming to a place of despair and hopelessness.

Fix your thoughts on what is true, and honorable, and right, and pure, and lovely, and admirable. Think about things that are excellent and worthy of praise. (Philippians 4:8b, NLT)

Thinking right is important to our entire wellbeing. The Lord told the Israelites to put His words into their hearts and minds, and to teach them to their children. He wanted them to do this so that they would continually think right! If we're constantly thinking positively, positive things will come out in our attitudes and actions. We will rejoice, pray, praise, declare, and speak what God is saying, because it will be in our heart and mind.

Therefore you shall lay up these My words in your [minds and] hearts and in your [entire] being, and bind them for a sign upon your hands and as forehead bands between your eyes.

And you shall teach them to your children, speaking of them when you sit in your house and when you walk along the road, when you lie down and when you rise up. (Deuteronomy 11:18–19, AMPC)

DAY 336

We Can't All Go but We Can All Pray

Recently I watched a video about an Indonesian Papuan tribe receiving Bibles that had been translated into their dialect for the first time. They truly are a thankful people, even though they have very little materially compared to us. They have something better: a great love for God, which they show with an enthusiasm and zeal that I have never seen in Canada. They show us by example that we don't need a lot of material things to be truly happy and satisfied—we just need the Lord.

I've been to Papua three times, and the Papuans are some of the most joyful, loving, caring, thankful, and zealous people I have ever had the pleasure of meeting. They hold a very special place in my heart. My son-in-law and granddaughter are Papuan. They are Indonesian but not tribal. Elijah's parents have given their entire lives to reaching the Papuan tribal people—in fact, Elijah's father was one of the first non-tribal people to live among the Papuans and bring the Good News to the remote village of Wamena. It has now grown into a small city located in the interior of the island in the Baliem Valley, and the only way in is by airplane.

Elijah told me that as a child he would walk for hours with his dad and brothers through the jungle to bring the Gospel to the different tribal villages. God has protected Elijah's family over the years in many dangerous situations. Papua really is the ends of the earth. Not everyone has the privilege of going, but everyone can pray and bless those who are able to go there and to many other parts of the world with the Gospel.

And this gospel of the kingdom will be preached in all the world as a witness to all the nations, and then the end will come. (Matthew 24:14, NKJV)

DAY 337

True Worship Comes from the Heart

True worship comes from the heart, and it's the driving force behind us moving forward in God—individually and corporately. When I think of true worship, the following scripture comes to mind where Jesus speaks to the Samaritan woman at the well.

> *God is Spirit, and those who worship Him must worship in spirit and truth.* (John 4:24, NKJV)

Webster's Dictionary defines worship as "To honor with extravagant love and extreme submission."[18] True worship affects the way we live; it is both an attitude and action. Worship is expressed not only through singing praises but by declaring God's Word, praying, giving, and serving. We worship God with our lives: not for what He can do, but for who He is. True worship comes from the inside out! It's internal—a matter of the heart—and it's rooted in the revelation of the truth of the revealed Word of God.

DAY 338

True Worship Is the Driving Force

True worship is the driving force that moves us forward in God! Synonyms for "driving force" listed on wordhippo.com are powerhouse, agent, motivator, dynamo, and spearhead.[19] Worship is the power and energy that motivates us to move forward in God—into what He has for us individually and corporately.

> ...saying with a loud voice: "Worthy is the Lamb who was slain to receive power and riches and wisdom, And strength and honor and glory and blessing!...Blessing and honor and glory and power be to Him who sits on the throne, And to the Lamb, forever and ever!" Then the four living creatures said, "Amen!" And the twenty-four elders fell down and worshipped Him who lives forever and ever. (Revelations 5:12, 13b–14, NKJV)

We always need to check our hearts and make sure that we are worshipping in spirit and in truth, as this is the driving force that will propel us forward into all that God has for us.

DAY 339

The Faithfulness of God

We can count on God, because He is always faithful! No matter what we're going through, there is no mountain too high or storm too great for the Lord to help us conquer. The Lord is always with us—whether in the fire, flood, or storm—and He's there in the midnight hour.

God is there whenever we need help. He will never take off or abandon us. He is faithful, our hope in every situation. We need to keep our minds fixed on His goodness and faithfulness and on how much He loves us; then, hope and faith will arise. Take His hand—He is there through it all.

> *But this I call to mind, and therefore I have hope:*
>
> *The steadfast love of the Lord never ceases; his mercies never come to an end; they are new every morning; great is your faithfulness. "The Lord is my portion," says my soul, "therefore I will hope in him."*
>
> *The Lord is good to those who wait for him, to the soul who seeks Him.* (Lamentations 3:21–25, ESV)

DAY 340

A Fruitful Tree

God wants each of us to be a fruitful tree in the House of the Lord. He wants us to plant ourselves in a church body and let our roots go deep. When we do this, we won't be bothered by circumstances or difficult seasons—no matter how long, intense, or hot they are. God doesn't want us to worry, but to put our hope and trust in Him.

People who choose to trust and make the Lord their hope will stay refreshed and restored, bearing fruit in good or hard times. They know God is good, and confidently put their hope and trust in Him. Spending time in the presence of the Lord, meditating on His word, and fellowshipping with other believers in times of worship will cause you to bear more fruit, and your faith will grow stronger.

But blessed are those who trust in the Lord and have made the Lord their hope and confidence. They are like trees planted along a riverbank, with roots that reach deep into the water. Such trees are not bothered by the heat or worried by long months of drought. Their leaves stay green, and they never stop producing fruit. (Jeremiah 17:7–8, NLT)

DAY 341

God Is Healing and Restoring Our Land

God is in the healing and restoring business. He wants to heal and restore this great country of Canada, as well as all the nations of the earth. It is His desire for all those who have gone astray to return to their first love and to be healed and restored.

It's our job as believers to pray and believe for this to take place. We must stand in faith, watching and believing like the father of the prodigal son did, until they all return.

> *Praise the Lord!*
>
> *How good it is to sing praises to our God! How delightful and how fitting! The Lord is rebuilding Jerusalem and bringing the exiles back to Israel. He heals the brokenhearted and bandages their wounds.... How great is our Lord! His power is absolute! His understanding is beyond comprehension!...*
>
> *Sing out your thanks to the Lord; sing praises to our God with a harp.... He takes no pleasure in the strength of a horse or in human might. No, the Lord's delight is in those who fear him, those who put their hope in his unfailing love.*
>
> *Glorify the Lord, O Jerusalem! Praise your God, O Zion! For He has strengthened the bars of your gates and blessed your children within your walls. He sends peace across your nation...* (Psalm 147:1–3, 5, 7, 10–14a, NLT)

He is the one who brings peace to your borders and satisfies your hunger with the finest wheat. He is the one who sends his promise throughout the earth. His word travels with great speed. (Psalm 147:14–15, GW)

DAY 342

Two Roots—Love or Fear

Every emotion has one of two roots—either love or fear. Science has shown us that we are wired for love and that we learn fear. We have the power to choose! In her book *The Gift in You*, Dr. Caroline Leaf says that, "In science, an attitude is a cluster of thoughts with emotions attached."[20]

It's always our choice whether we will react to circumstances and trials with love or fear. Thoughts have feelings of either fear or love attached to them, and all other emotions stem from them. Emotions rooted in love bring life, and those rooted in fear bring death. Everything starts out as a thought, and then it becomes a spoken word, action, and/or attitude.

Death and life are in the power of the tongue… (Proverbs 18:21a, NKJV)

I call heaven and earth as witnesses today against you, that I have set before you life and death, blessing and cursing; therefore choose life, that both you and your descendants may live… (Deuteronomy 30:19, NKJV)

When we to choose to think rightly, we speak and act with a correct heart attitude. Negative attitudes and actions will bring about wrong results in our lives, such as anger, bitterness, unforgiveness, hatred, depression, and addictions. Positive attitudes and actions will result in love, joy, peace, forgiveness, and freedom. Choose to think positively, which is living God's way, and you will have a good outcome.

DAY 343

Live in the Love Channel

How we think really does affect how we react to the circumstances and difficulties we face. That's why identical twins with the same genetic makeup can grow up in the same environment, but react to life in such different ways. It depends on how we think and deal with the circumstances of our lives, good or bad. If a set of identical twins were both abused as children and one decides to forgive, that twin will walk in love and freedom and have success, while the other twin will likely struggle in many areas of life. It all depends on how we choose to think and react to life—either with love or fear.

The Bible tells us in 1 John 4:18 (NKJV) that *"...perfect love casts out fear, because fear involves torment."* Fear will bring torment to the mind when we choose to entertain wrong thoughts, but when we make the decision to meditate on things that are good, love will prevail.

We were made in love—created by God, who *is* Love. We can live in the love channel, but living in fear is a learned response. Choose what kind of life you'll live—one filled with fear, or one filled with love.

God is our refuge and strength, A very present help in trouble. Therefore we will not fear, Even though the earth be removed, And though the mountains be carried into the midst of the sea; Though its waters roar and be troubled, Though the mountains shake with its swelling. There is a river whose streams shall make glad the city of God, The holy place of the tabernacle of the Most High. God is in the midst of her; she shall not be moved....

Be still, and know that I am God; I will be exalted among the nations, I will be exalted in the earth!...

The Lord of Hosts is with us; The God of Jacob is our refuge.
(Psalm 46:1–5a, 10, 12, NKJV)

DAY 344

Let His Spirit Rise within You

We have the freedom to choose whom we spend our time with. When we choose the Lord, His desires will become ours as we allow His Spirit to rise within us. Whether we will walk according to our fleshly desires or the Spirit of God is our choice.

> *God's Spirit makes us loving, happy, peaceful, patient, kind, good, faithful, gentle, and self-controlled. There is no law against behaving in any of these ways. And because we belong to Christ Jesus, we have killed our selfish feelings and desires. God's Spirit has given us life, and so we should follow the Spirit.* (Galatians 5:22–25, CEV)

Choose life and let His Spirit rise within you.

DAY 345

Words from Heaven

I was praying with a couple of ladies when the Lord started talking to us about how he was opening up the books of heaven to us—manna from heaven, the Bread of Life. The books God was speaking about are those in which He has written the plans, purposes, and destinies for each of our lives, as well as those of churches, cities, and nations. The Lord has always wanted us to know what is written in those books, but we haven't always been in position to hear.

I believe that things are going to begin to be revealed to us individually and as churches. This will happen when we seek Him, letting His light reveal the wonderful words He has written in those books—plans that He has had for us since before the foundation of the world. Psalm 40 speaks of these books.

> He taught me how to sing the latest God-song, a praise-song to our God. More and more people are seeing this: they enter the mystery, abandoning themselves to God.
>
> Blessed are you who give yourselves over to God, turn your backs on the world's "sure thing," ignore what the world worships; The world's a huge stockpile of God-wonders and God-thoughts. Nothing and no one comes close to you! I start talking about you, telling what I know, and quickly run out of words. Neither numbers nor words account for you.
>
> Doing something for you, bringing something to you—that's not what you're after. Being religious, acting pious—that's not what you're asking for. You've opened my ears so I can listen. (Psalm 40:3–6, MSG)

And so, I said, "I am here to do what is written about me in the book," where it says, "I enjoy pleasing you. Your law is in my heart." (Psalm 40:7–8, CEV)

DAY 346

Choices Are Thoughts Acted Out

Choices are thoughts acted out. When I think of choices, the song "I Choose to Believe" by Phillips, Craig and Dean comes to mind. This song also includes the words "Jesus, Jesus, how I trust Him; How I've proved Him over and over; Jesus, Jesus, precious Jesus; Oh for grace to trust Him more," taken from the hymn "Tis so Sweet to Trust in Jesus." After my husband passed away, I sang and listened to these words over and over, as they really ministered to me.

When I suddenly found myself in a new season, I made up my mind right then that God was good and my trust would remain in Him. Life is all about choices!

Oh, taste and see that the Lord is good; Blessed is the man who trusts in Him! (Psalm 34:8, NKJV)

As for God, His way is perfect; The word of the Lord is proven; He is a shield to all who trust in Him. (2 Samuel 22:31, NKJV)

DAY 347
Listen for That Still Small Voice

We have all let the cares of this life overwhelm us at times. Even when things are going well, we're receiving answers to our prayers, and we seem to be moving forward in our lives, we can still become anxious, worried, or apprehensive. This happens because change is never easy, and it brings new challenges and new decisions. Even when we know we've made the right decision, we can feel like we're stuck in the mud with our wheels spinning, and we quickly find ourselves saying, "Lord, now what?"

That's what happened to me when I sold my acreage. I was very excited to move on, but there were a lot of decisions to be made. For the first time in many years, I had to make a major life-changing decision all on my own.

Situations like this make you realize how dependent you are on the Lord, and how much you need His wisdom and guidance. The devil will try to bombard you with all kinds of negative thoughts and confusion. Fortunately, God reminded me during that time to listen to His still small voice. His voice is bigger and louder than any other; even though it is small and quiet, it can be heard clearly over any storm. We have to trust and give all of our worries and concerns to Him. Let Him lead, knowing He will get us through to the other side.

> *Casting the whole of your care [all your anxieties, all your worries, all your concerns, once and for all] on Him, for He cares for you affectionately and cares about you watchfully.*
>
> *Be well balanced (temperate, sober of mind), be vigilant and cautious at all times; for that enemy of yours, the devil, roams around like a lion roaring [in fierce hunger], seeking someone to seize upon and devour.*

Withstand him; be firm in faith [against his onset—rooted, established, strong, immovable, and determined]....

And after you have suffered a little while, the God of all grace [Who imparts all blessing and favor], Who has called you to His [own] eternal glory in Christ Jesus, will Himself complete and make you what you ought to be, establish and ground you securely, and strengthen, and settle you. (1 Peter 5:7–9a, 10, AMPC)

DAY 348

Touched by the River

God is amazing. His timing is perfect—He knows exactly what we need and when. The Lord will move every mountain out of our way if we will believe. It doesn't matter what the situation looks like—there is nothing God can't do. When we find ourselves in a situation that seems impossible, just stay in faith. It's never over until it's over.

A small group of us were praying one evening, and we began calling out on behalf of people we knew who had strayed away from the Lord or were just not giving their all to serve Him. They were teetering on the edge, saying, "Should I or shouldn't I live for and serve God?" We started praying that they would walk in the light of His glory, and that the river of God would flow in their lives, sweeping them into His Kingdom.

Ezekiel 47 came to mind as we prayed. This passage speaks of the river of God flowing from the Temple into the Dead Sea, describing how everything lives wherever the water flows. The sea in Scripture often refers to people—the sea of humanity. There is a sea of dead humanity—they're physically alive but spiritually dead. When they get touched by His glory—His presence—they'll be saved and restored once again. This river restores, refreshes, and renews. The chapter goes on in to say that the Dead Sea will be filled with all kinds of fish. God is bringing in people of every colour, race, tribe, nationality, culture, and religion.

> *There will be swarms of living things wherever the water of this river flows. Fish will abound in the Dead Sea, for its waters will become fresh. Life will flourish wherever this water flows. Fishermen will stand along the shores of the Dead Sea. All the way from En-gedi to En-eglaim, the shores will be covered with nets drying in the sun. Fish of every kind will fill the Dead Sea, just as they fill the Mediterranean.* (Ezekiel 47:9–10, NLT)

DAY 349
It's Time to Rally the Troops

There are several churches in our province that have been getting together for two or three conferences a year. These same churches gathered together and had two praise nights in different cities in our province. It is very exciting to see churches uniting and worshipping together.

> ...not forsaking the assembling of ourselves together, as is the manner of some, but exhorting one another, and so much the more as you see the Day approaching. (Hebrews 10:25, NKJV)

The above scripture is talking about the whole Body of Christ. We are one Church, one body, and one army. It's time to rally the troops and march together as one. An army has several divisions and specialty squadrons, each with their own unique assignment. However, they still must work together to accomplish their goals. The goal of any army is to defeat the enemy and take the land.

An army is a powerful, undefeatable force when it operates the way God designed it to. For any army to succeed it must operate in unity, each division helping the other. Soldiers are dependent on each other—they don't go into battle alone. Lone rangers are targeted quickly, but there is power, protection, and safety in numbers. When churches come together in praise and worship, lifting the Name of Jesus, it changes the atmosphere over cities and regions and it causes the enemy to flee. It sets us up to invade the enemy's territory and take possession of the land.

DAY 350

Unity Produces Synergy

Unity among churches sets us up to defeat the enemy and to take the land. We are the army of God divided into different regiments or divisions. When we come together to pray or praise, we produce a synergy that changes the atmosphere over cities and regions.

"Synergy" is defined by the Oxford Dictionary as "The interaction or cooperation of two or more organizations, substances, or other agents to produce a combined effect greater than the sum of their separate effects."[21] Some synonyms for synergy listed on thesaurus.com are alliance, harmony, unity, and teamwork.[22] The Church is rising as a united force and producing a synergy, which will enable it to defeat the enemy and possess the land.

> *See how good and pleasant it is when brothers and sisters live together in harmony! It is like fine, scented oil on the head, running down the beard—down Aaron's beard—running over the collar of his robes. It is like dew on Mount Hermon, dew which comes down on Zion's mountains. That is where the Lord promised the blessing of eternal life.* (Psalm 133, GW)

DAY 351

Rejoicing—A Necessary Part of Life

A person can rejoice their way through anything! The more we rejoice and praise, the more resilient we become to life's circumstances. "Resilient" according to dictionary.com means "springing back; rebounding... returning to the original form or position after being bent, compressed, or stretched... recovering readily from illness, depression, adversity, or the like; buoyant."[23]

> We often suffer, but we are never crushed. Even when we don't know what to do, we never give up. In times of trouble, God is with us, and when we are knocked down, we get up again. (2 Corinthians 4:8–9, CEV)

Keep rejoicing, praying, and pressing into God's presence, and you will become more and more resilient, springing back quickly from hard times.

DAY 352

The Voice of Praise Will Overcome Anything

Praise is a vital part of a Christian's life. Praise opens up the heavens over our lives, and there is nothing we can't praise our way through. Praising will bring victory and freedom. All we need to do is rejoice and say something good about God, and peace and joy will begin to rise from within. It's the sound of faith, and it will bring freedom and victory to our lives.

God is good all the time, and there is no storm that the voice of praise cannot overcome. God brought the victory to Paul and Silas because they chose to praise Him. God brought victory to the Israelites many times through their praises. All they had to do was shout when God said "Shout," and the walls came down and they won the battle.

I know from personal experience that praise can help you through the most difficult of times. When I was told that my husband had gone to heaven, the first thing I heard from God was "Praise Me!" I turned and told my friend Pat, "God said to praise Him, so we need to praise Him and keep praising Him." We did that all the way back to Saskatoon. We just kept saying, "God is good—no matter what," and we chose to put on the garment of praise.

The Bible tells us to always rejoice, and so we need to wear our garment of praise continually. Praise is rejoicing in the Lord for who He is, for what He has done, is doing, and will do. We taught a song called "My God My King," written by Leslie Jordan and David Leonard, to the Kenyan children, and we sang it over and over on our way home. This simple little song talks about how if we will sing and keep on singing to

God, everything else will melt away. It also tells us we should love the Lord with all our heart because He is always good.

Oh, give thanks to the Lord, for He is good! For His mercy endures forever. (1 Chronicles 16:34, NKJV)

Oh, taste and see that the Lord is good; Blessed is the man who trusts in Him! (Psalm 34:8, NKJV)

I will bless the Lord at all times; His praise shall continually be in my mouth. (Psalm 34:1, NKJV)

DAY 353

Cultivate a Lifestyle of Praise and Prayer

God is good, and sometimes we just need to sit and reflect on what He has done in our lives. Recently, I found myself reflecting on everything that had happened over the past few years. I had to deal with some unexpected and very difficult trials. I thought about how I had responded and how others had reacted, and why some people seem to be able to go through hard times and come out of it stronger than ever while others struggle. I believe it all has to do with choices—not only those we make during the storm, but the ones we make before any difficulties arise. We need to cultivate a lifestyle of praise and prayer, because if we haven't learned to, it will be that much more of a struggle to do so during hard times. If we learn to act on the Word of God, we will experience the results of that choice.

> *Rejoice always, pray without ceasing, in everything give thanks; for this is the will of God in Christ Jesus for you.* (1 Thessalonians 5:16–18, NKJV)

We can't keep changing our minds, thinking God's way and then the world's way—that is being double-minded. We must choose to think rightly, no matter what circumstance we find ourselves in. Choose to be glad, and you won't be sad or mad.

> *My brethren, count it all joy when you fall into various trials…* (James 1:2, NKJV)

We need to rejoice and be thankful at all times, knowing God is right there with us. He is a good Father. No matter what happens, only good comes from Him. He is right there through every season of our life.

My friends, be glad, even if you have a lot of trouble. You know that you learn to endure by having your faith tested. But you must learn to endure everything, so that you will be completely mature and not lacking in anything....
But when you ask for something, you must have faith and not doubt. Anyone who doubts is like an ocean wave tossed around in a storm. If you are that kind of person, you can't make up your mind, and you surely can't be trusted. So don't expect the Lord to give you anything at all. (James 1:2–4, 6–8, CEV)

DAY 354

Character Matters

House hunting can be quite an adventure, but we can learn so much from the experience. When I was looking to purchase a different home, I looked at several early twentieth-century homes. Character homes are my favourite style of house. Older homes that have been taken care of are beautiful—it was just a matter of finding one with the right kind of character that had been well-maintained.

Character is important in many aspects of life, especially godly character. We need to take care of our own spiritual house and make sure we are doing the upkeep on it: renewing it with the Word, restoring it through repentance when necessary, refreshing it with His presence, cleaning and dusting it of wrong thoughts and actions whenever needed, and letting His character shine through.

It can be trying when we have to step into a new season or face difficulties, but trials enable us to develop patience and faith. We learn to persevere, knowing that God's grace and favour are working on our behalf. The experience matures us and shows forth our character. When difficulties arise, what's in us will come out.

> *Through Christ we can approach God and stand in his favor. So we brag because of our confidence that we will receive glory from God. But that's not all. We also brag when we are suffering. We know that suffering creates endurance, endurance creates character, and character creates confidence. We're not ashamed to have this confidence, because God's love has been poured into our hearts by the Holy Spirit...* (Romans 5:2–5, GW)

DAY 355

The Spirit of the Lord Is Invading

One day I was driving and praying over the city of Saskatoon, and I got very excited in my spirit. I sensed that something is about to break forth—not just in Saskatoon, Saskatchewan, or Canada, but around the world. It will be like nothing we have ever heard or seen. There have been great moves of God in the past, right here in Saskatoon and other places, but we haven't seen anything like we're going to see in the days ahead. It will happen as we pray, praise, and lift up Jesus' Name.

The Spirit of the Lord is invading cities, regions and nations. The atmosphere is changing as people pray and praise! It will be like when men such as Smith Wigglesworth held revival meetings and people would come within a few blocks of where they had gathered: the Spirit of God would invade their lives, and they would repent and get saved. This is what came to me: "As soon as planes touch the soil or vehicles enter the city, people are going to be overwhelmed and invaded by the presence of the Holy Spirit." People are going to be drawn to the Lord because of His light, presence, and glory, and this will draw back many who have fallen away.

God has set cities, regions, and nations apart to shine forth His glory. There are those who struggle to believe that this could really happen—but I believe it will, and sooner than we think. Can a city or even a nation be saved in a day? Yes, it can—if only we will believe!

> *Arise, shine, for your light has come, and the glory of the Lord rises upon you. See, darkness covers the earth and thick darkness is over the peoples, but the Lord rises upon you and his glory appears over you. Nations will come to your light, and kings to the brightness of your dawn.*

Lift up your eyes and look about you: All assemble and come to you; your sons come from afar, and your daughters are carried on the hip. Then you will look and be radiant, your heart will throb and swell with joy; the wealth on the seas will be brought to you, to you the riches of the nations will come. (Isaiah 60:1–5, NIV)

DAY 356

The Benefits of Praise

Praise has many benefits—among them, it will get us through any difficulty life throws our way. When we praise God, it takes our focus off ourselves and fixes it on the Lord. It helps us see the good in everything, it causes rejoicing and thankfulness to erupt out of us with shouts of joy, and it changes the atmosphere in the heavens and in our hearts.

Make a joyful shout to God, all the earth! Sing out the honor of His name; Make His praise glorious....
   Oh bless our God, you peoples! And make the voice of His praise to be heard... (Psalm 66:1–2, 8, NKJV)

Let the peoples praise You, O God; Let all the peoples praise you. (Psalm 67:3, NKJV)

DAY 357

Praise Positions Us for Victory

One day the Lord impressed upon me the importance of being in the right position. He told me that positioning is key, and that we need to position ourselves for victory. Then this thought come to my mind: "Praise positions us for victory."

In 2 Chronicles 20, Jehoshaphat sought the Lord concerning the armies that were coming against his forces, and God told him to put the singers out in front of the army. By putting them first, he positioned the Israelites for victory!

> *And when he had consulted with the people, he appointed those who should sing to the Lord, and who should praise the beauty of holiness, as they went out before the army and were saying:*
>
> *"Praise the Lord, For His mercy endures forever."*
>
> *Now when they began to sing and to praise, the Lord set ambushes against the people of Ammon, Moab, and Mount Seir, who had come against Judah; and they were defeated.* (2 Chronicles 20:21–22, NKJV)

Praise will position us for victory, personally and corporately. Paul and Silas praised their way to victory. We can do the same for ourselves and together as churches, cities, regions, and nations.

DAY 358

The Four Corners

I was praying one evening with a small group of ladies about the twenty-four-hour prayer and praise services that had been taking place in our city, and the Lord said to me the words, "Four corners." He showed me a picture of an X with four different groups of people—one group standing on each corner. As I saw this picture in my mind, the vision that Peter had experienced while he was praying on his rooftop came to mind.

> ...he fell into a trance and saw heaven opened and an object like a great sheet bound at the four corners, descending to him and let down to the earth. In it were all kinds of four-footed animals of the earth, wild beasts, creeping things, and birds of the air. And a voice came to him, "Rise, Peter; kill and eat."
> But Peter said, "Not so, Lord! For I have never eaten anything common or unclean."
> And a voice spoke to him again the second time, "What God has cleansed you must not call common." (Acts 10:10b–15, NKJV)

This is what I believe God was saying: the four corners represent four different groups of people. As we praise, it is changing the atmosphere and the hearts of the people in all four of these groups. The first group is the Christians, and as we lift up Jesus' Name it will bring restoration and refreshing to our lives and draw us closer to the Lord. The second group is the prodigals—those who have wandered away. The third group is the religious, and the fourth group is the unchurched—those who have never heard or learned anything about God. They are coming from these four corners to intersect at the centre.

Jesus is the centre! In Peter's vision, he heard a voice say, "Kill and eat." People from all four groups are coming to the Lord, and are going to die to self, take up their cross, and follow Jesus. They are coming to the banqueting table of His presence, where they will eat of Him. As praise fills the atmosphere it will affect everyone, including those doing the praising. It's positioning our city and nation for salvation and victory.

DAY 359

Dressed in Praise

I will bless the Lord at all times; His praise shall continually be in my mouth. (Psalm 34:1, NKJV)

Be glad in the Lord and rejoice, you righteous; And shout for joy, all you upright in heart! (Psalm 32:11, NKJV)

Every morning, we need to rise up and dress ourselves in praise. The Bible says in Isaiah 61:3 (NKJV) that the Lord has given us *"...the garment of praise...,"* but we have to choose every day to wear it.

We need to put on praise—no matter the circumstance. In the natural realm, it doesn't matter what season it is—we still have to put on our clothes. We don't leave home undressed, and we shouldn't start our day without clothing ourselves in praise.

Rejoice in the Lord always. Again I will say, rejoice! (Philippians 4:4, NKJV)

Rejoice always... (1 Thessalonians 5:16, NKJV)

Continual praising will keep our minds constantly fixed on the Lord. When we stay focused on the Lord, no matter the difficulties, it will be impossible to stay sad, depressed, miserable, or unhappy. Praise brings us into the very throne room of God. In His presence we will find joy and strength, enabling us to endure whatever comes our way. Always remember to start each day with praise!

DAY 360

I Can Do All Things

I woke up one morning with the following scripture from the book of Philippians on my mind.

I can do all things through Christ who strengthens me. (Philippians 4:13, NKJV)

Then the thought came: we must think correctly to be able to do all things. If I think I can't do it, then I won't be able to. When I was young, I did well in math until I had to learn algebra. I found it difficult to understand, and I developed a bad attitude. I decided math was too difficult and that I was no good at it. I quit taking math courses as soon as it wasn't a requirement anymore. When I was sixteen, I took driver's education and the instructor said I was a very good driver, but I failed the road test three times. I developed a belief that I would never pass, and it was several years later before I took a road test again. I'd had a change of attitude, and I passed easily.

If God places something in our hearts that He wants us to do, then we need to believe that He will enable us to accomplish it. He won't ask us to do something He hasn't given us the ability to do. In Philippians chapter 4, the verses before verse 13 are interesting in light of that verse.

Rejoice in the Lord always. Again I will say, rejoice! (Philippians 4:4, NKJV)

Don't worry about anything; instead, pray about everything. Tell God what you need, and thank him for all he has done. Then you will experience God's peace, which exceeds anything we can understand. His peace will guard your hearts and minds as you live in Christ Jesus. (Philippians 4:6–7, NLT)

And now, dear brothers and sisters, one final thing. Fix your thoughts on what is true, and honorable, and right, and pure, and lovely, and admirable. Think about things that are excellent and worthy of praise. (Philippians 4:8, NLT)

Paul goes on to thank the Philippians for giving to him, and describes how he has learned the secret of being content in every circumstance.

I can endure all these things through the power of the one who gives me strength. (Philippians 4:13, CEB)

We receive the strength to endure anything by doing what was said in the earlier verses: rejoice always, pray, be thankful, and fix your thoughts on right things; then "I can't" will become your "I can!" "*I can* do all things through Christ who strengthens me!"

DAY 361

He Will Perfect That Which Concerns You

I sold my acreage and was looking for a character house to buy. Eventually, I had looked at so many that my mind was overloaded and I wasn't sure which one I should put an offer on. So I settled myself down and said, "Okay, this is what I want, Lord—I'm asking you to find me the right house."

This is what He said to me: "I have the perfect house for you: it's the perfect size, in the perfect location, at the perfect price, because I've perfected that which concerns you." When we make the choice to allow the Lord to work on our behalf, leaving it in His hands, things will always work out perfectly, because God is good and He only has good things for us.

> *The Lord will perfect that which concerns me…* (Psalm 138:8a, NKJV)

> *It is God who arms me with strength, And makes my way perfect.* (Psalm 18:32, NKJV)

> *As for God, His way is perfect; The word of the Lord is proven; He is a shield to all who trust in Him. …*
> *God is my strength and power, And He makes my way perfect.* (2 Samuel 22:31, 33, NKJV)

DAY 362

Never Settle for Less Than God's Best

While looking to purchase a character home, I learned some things through the whole process—primarily that God knows best. He knew what I desired in a home and what I needed, and His timing was perfect. I put an offer in on two different houses, but neither one had everything that I had asked the Lord for in a house. I was disappointed because the owners of the first house didn't accept my offer, and I discovered that the foundation wasn't good on the second one.

I learned two valuable lessons. First, don't ever compromise. When you ask your Heavenly Father for something, never settle for less. He wants to give you what you ask for—and He had the right house for me, which met all my needs perfectly. Secondly, not everything is as it appears: the second house was built on a poor foundation. It's similar with people—it can seem like all is good and they have everything together, but if their lives aren't built on a strong foundation, at some point there's going to be a collapse or cave in. We need to make sure that we build our life on Christ, the cornerstone, our sure foundation!

These words I speak to you are not mere additions to your life, homeowner improvements to your standard of living. They are foundation words, words to build a life on.

If you work the words into your life, you are like a smart carpenter who dug deep and laid the foundation of his house on bedrock. When the river burst its banks and crashed against the house, nothing could shake it; it was built to last. But if you just use my words in Bible studies and don't work them into your life, you are like a dumb carpenter who built a house but skipped the foundation. When the swollen river came crashing in, it collapsed like a house of cards. It was a total loss. (Luke 6:47–49, MSG)

DAY 363

Feed on His Faithfulness

What we feed our natural bodies is important, as the foods we consume affect each of us differently. There are certain foods that my body doesn't tolerate very well, and if I eat them my stomach gets upset and I end up with a headache. Our bodies can't perform at their best when we fill them with things that aren't good for them, and this will affect our service to the Lord.

It's even more important what we allow our spirits to feed on—it may not be sin, but a weight that isn't good for us even if it's fine for someone else. We must be careful what we fill our minds and hearts with.

Trust in the Lord, and do good; Dwell in the land, and feed on His faithfulness. (Psalm 37:3, NKJV)

…let us also lay aside any weight, and sin which clings so closely, and let us run with endurance the race that is set before us… (Hebrews 12:1b, ESV)

DAY 364

Praise Changes the Atmosphere

From the time I was a young child, I have always liked to listen to music. As a young adult I owned over one hundred music albums, and even though I never thought of myself as a singer, I loved to sing along whenever I played those records. When I got saved and really began paying attention to the words in the songs, I quickly realized that they weren't good. All they sang about was drugs, drinking and drunkenness, suicide, and all kinds of other negative things, none of which built up or encouraged anyone.

I recognized that the music had a negative influence, so I decided with the help of my roommate to smash them all and throw them in the garbage. I was just going to throw them away, but she said, "No—if we do that someone will just take them out of the garbage and keep them." They weren't easy to break, and we had to throw and stomp on them before they broke.

It's not easy sometimes to get rid of or break free from things that are negative influences or harmful. But God always has something better—I went from rock and roll to praise and worship music. We travelled often from where I was living to the farm owned by the parents of my then-fiancé, Clarence, and we would listen to and sing praise songs all the time. I learned early on that praise lifts us up and brings us into the Lord's presence, and that we don't have to be a singer to praise, but we can't praise without singing. God wants us to have fun in His presence, and we had lots of good times singing and praising Him in those days.

God gets enjoyment from being with us and wants us to enjoy being with Him. There's nothing like the presence of the King! Praise brings you through the courts of the palace right into the throne room. The Holy Spirit is a singing Spirit, so when we start singing and praising, His Spirit begins rising up within us.

When our spirit takes the lead, we won't be controlled by our thoughts, emotions, or flesh. John said he was in the Spirit on the Lord's Day, and he heard and saw. When we allow our spirit to take control, we will see and hear what God is saying about today and tomorrow. Things are revealed in God's presence and His Word comes alive to us, causing revelation and understanding to come. Freedom, joy, victory, and salvation are the results of spending time in His presence.

Praise brought freedom to Paul and Silas and all the prisoners, and it brought salvation to the jailer and his whole household. Praise will bring freedom, salvation, and victory to every area of our life, and it will disperse darkness and change the atmosphere over churches, cities, regions, and nations. Let the sound of praise rise from within you! It's a sound of faith, freedom, victory, and rejoicing! It will set the captives free, send the enemy fleeing, and bring freedom and salvation. You can praise your way through anything, but it's even more powerful when you praise with others, because it produces synergy!

Praise the Lord! Sing to the Lord a new song, And His praise in the assembly of saints. Let Israel rejoice in their Maker; Let the children of Zion be joyful in their King. Let them praise His name with the dance; Let them sing praises to Him with the timbrel and harp. For the Lord takes pleasure in His people; He will beautify the humble with salvation. Let the saints be joyful in glory; Let them sing aloud on their beds. Let the high praises of God be in their mouth, And a two-edged sword in their hand... (Psalm 149:1–6, NKJV)

DAY 365

Endowed with Strength

One day I was sitting in my car, listening to music and thinking about the Joy of the Lord. His joy has kept me and strengthened me through difficulties. It has empowered me to go through the floodwaters and not drown. It's the wave that has carried me deeper into His presence and overwhelmed me.

When we are filled with joy, we experience an overwhelming emotion that brings strength and only comes from His presence. Worship brings us into the place of fullness of joy where we are safe, free, and at peace—nothing this world offers can take its place, and no storm can take it from us. If we allow it, the trials of life will increase that joy; it will endow us with strength to overcome anything. Choose to allow the Lord to fill you with His joy and strength!

...and in Christ you have been brought to fullness. (Colossians 2:10a, NIV)

And you have been filled by him... (Colossians 2:10a, CEB)

DAY 366

Remove the Waterline

A few years ago I woke up in the middle of the night and heard very clearly, "Remove the waterline." The only reference I had to this point of a waterline was my husband: Clarence had been a plumber, and always referred to pipes as waterlines. The only other understanding I had of a waterline was a mark left on a wall indicating how high the floodwaters had come. I looked up the word "waterline" and discovered at Wikipedia that "the waterline is the line where the hull of ship meets the surface of the water... a special marking... (positioned amidships), that indicates the draft of the ship and the legal limit to which a ship may be loaded for specific water types and temperatures in order to safely maintain buoyancy...."[24] The waterline is very important in ensuring that the ship isn't overloaded, which would cause it to sink.

This scripture came immediately to my mind:

> *He walked to the east with a measuring tape and measured off fifteen hundred feet, leading me through water that was ankle-deep. He measured off another fifteen hundred feet, leading me through water that was knee-deep. He measured off another fifteen hundred feet, leading me through water waist-deep. He measured off another fifteen hundred feet. By now it was a river over my head, water to swim in, water no one could possible walk through.* (Ezekiel 47:3–5, MSG)

I asked the Lord for clarification on what He was saying to me. This is what rose out of my spirit: It's time to get in over our heads, and for an overload of the Holy Spirit. It's time to fill our vessels to capacity and to take off the limits. No more waterlines. No more ankle-deep, knee-deep, or waist-deep times in His presence. It's time to go all the way and start swimming. There is no limit to where the Holy Spirit can take us! An overloaded ship will sink below the waterline, so the waterline is very necessary, but in a spiritual context it limits us to how deep we can or will go. We need to remove the waterline from the radar screen of our thinking and realize we can never go too deep into God's presence.

Recently the Lord reminded me of this vision, but this time He said, "Remove any trace of the waterline from your life." My first thought was of a chalkboard where the line had been erased, but a faint line still appeared. It's time to take off every limit, and remove it so there is no trace left.

The Lord told me that once we believers get rid of the limitations preventing us from going where the Spirit wants to take us, and once we completely eradicate the waterline-limitations in our lives, all those who will believe will experience a gusher! He said these words to me: "Get ready for a gusher." I looked up the meaning, and Oxford Dictionaries defines "gusher" as "An oil well from which oil flows profusely without being pumped."[25] I know that "profusely" means "excessively" or "in a large capacity." So if we will remove the waterline in our lives, the Holy Spirit is going to flow unhindered through us like a gusher.

ENDNOTES

[1] https://en.oxforddictionaries.com/definition/irresistible, accessed January 18, 2019.

[2] http://www.wordreference.com/definition/entirely, accessed January 18, 2019.

[3] Dick Eastman, *Intercessory Worship: Combining Worship & Prayer to Touch the Heart of God* (Ventura, CA: Regal/Gospel Light, 2002), p. 27.

[4] https://www.merriam-webster.com/dictionary/extravaganza, accessed January 18, 2019.

[5] https://www.urbandictionary.com/define.php?term=extravaganza&utm_source=search-action, accessed January 18, 2019.

[6] Dick Eastman, *Intercessory Worship*, p. 161.

[7] https://en.oxforddictionaries.com/definition/resurrect, accessed January 19, 2019.

[8] https://www.synonym.com/synonyms/resurrect, accessed January 19, 2019.

[9] https://www.dictionary.com/browse/miscarriage, accessed January 19, 2019.

[10] http://www.businessdictionary.com/definition/synergy.html, accessed January 19, 2019.

[11] https://www.yourdictionary.com/self-made, accessed January 19, 2019.

[12] https://en.oxforddictionaries.com/definition/adversity, accessed January 20, 2019.

[13] https://www.dictionary.com/browse/adversity, accessed January 20, 2019.

[14] https://www.thesaurus.com/browse/all-consuming, accessed January 20, 2019.

[15] https://www.dictionary.com/browse/continually, accessed January 20, 2019.

[16] Caroline Leaf, *The Gift in You* (Nashville, TN: Thomas Nelson, 2009), p. 174.

[17] John Bevere. *Extraordinary: The Life You're Meant to Live* (Colorado Springs, CO: WaterBrook Press, 2014), p. 4.

[18] http://webstersdictionary1828.com/Dictionary/worship, accessed March 9, 2019.

[19] https://www.wordhippo.com/what-is/another-word-for/driving_force.html, accessed January 21, 2019.

[20] Caroline Leaf, *The Gift in You*, p. 139.

[21] https://en.oxforddictionaries.com/definition/synergy, accessed January 22, 2019.

[22] https://www.thesaurus.com/browse/synergy, accessed January 22, 2019.

[23] https://www.dictionary.com/browse/resilient, accessed January 22, 2019.

[24] https://en.wikipedia.org/wiki/Waterline, accessed March 17, 2019.

[25] https://en.oxforddictionaries.com/definition/gusher, accessed March 17, 2019.

OTHER BOOKS BY LORNA HANISHEWSKI

Devotions of the Heart, Book One
ISBN: 978-1-4866-1781-4
eBook ISBN: 978-1-4866-1782-1

Devotions of the Heart, Book One is the first book in a two-book series. It contains six months' worth of devotionals, written from the acquired wisdom, knowledge, and understanding of scripture that Lorna has obtained through times of prayer, praise, and study of God's Word. Each devotional touches on a wide range of topics that are sure to uplift your soul and inspire you to develop a closer relationship with the Lord as you read and meditate.

Topics include:
- Prayer
- Praise
- God's Presence
- Leading by the Spirit
- Freedom in Christ
- Hope
- Overcoming fear, sorrow, and grief

Be encouraged and uplifted as Devotions of the Heart helps you develop even greater intimacy with the Lord.

Pure Joy

Print ISBN: 978-1-4866-1779-1
eBook ISBN: 978-1-4866-1780-7

Joy is a sustaining force in the Christian life, giving us strength to endure the most difficult of circumstances. Grieving the death of her husband by suicide, and facing other life tragedies, Lorna Hanishewski discovered that great joy can be experienced in a relationship with Jesus Christ. Founded on the truths of the Word of God, this practical book identifies seven keys to accessing true Christian joy. The pages are filled with biblical and personal examples of how to live a joy-filled life, challenging and inspiring readers to take hold of this fruit of the Spirit available to all who believe.